THEATRE GAMES FOR YOUNG PERFORMERS

Improvisations & Exercises for Developing Acting Skills

MARIA C. NOVELLY

MERIWETHER PUBLISHING LTD.
Colorado Springs, Colorado

Meriwether Publishing Ltd., Publisher
Box 7710
Colorado Springs, CO 80933-7710

Executive Editor: Arthur Zapel
Designer: Michelle Z. Gallardo
Photographer: Gene Knudsen
Indexer: Dana Mottweiler

© Copyright MCMLXXXV Meriwether Publishing Ltd.
Printed in the United States of America
First Edition

Library of Congress Cataloging-in-Publication Data

Novelly, Maria C.
      Theatre games for young performers : improvisa-
tions & exercises for developing acting skills / by
Maria C. Novelly. — 1st ed. — Colorado Springs, CO :
Meriwether Pub., c1985

      147 p. : ill. ; 23 cm.

      Includes index.
      ISBN 0-916260-31-3 (pbk.)

      1. Drama in education.   2. Acting—Study and
teaching. 3. Theater and youth. I. Title.
PN3171.N67   1985   792'.07'1273—dc19   85-60572
                              AACR 2 MARC

10 11 12   01 02 03

For Toni and Walt

ACKNOWLEDGEMENTS

*I would like to acknowledge the following people
for their help and insight in preparing this book:
Gary Frier, who suggested I try out his Applewriter;
Roz Russell-Turk, who suggested I "keep it simple;"
Nancy Driscoll, for general moral support;
Emi Mueller and Suzy Tomasovic, for wit and criticism.
I would also like to mention Alma Dinwiddie, whose students
I continued to borrow after I began teaching older teens;
Fran Everidge, whose inspiration I have drawn on
in the years since I was her student;
and two mime artists, Paul Hanel and Karl Metzger,
whose energy and creativity I found uplifting.
Finally, my thanks to the many drama instructors and coaches
I have worked with; and most of all, my gratitude
to my junior high-school students, all of whom had their
great moments on the stage.*

TABLE of CONTENTS

*Many exercises are followed by samples of actor worksheets. For greater ease in finding specific exercises, consult the Index to Activities, and then look for headings like this one:

Believable Entrances

INTRODUCTION

This book contains dramatic activities that have been devised, adapted and used with success with adolescent performers.

Not a textbook for performers, this book serves as a resource for drama teachers and coaches, Scout leaders, church youth leaders, and recreational and camp directors. Any classroom teacher or group leader who wants to incorporate drama into an educational, recreational or religious program will find this book concise and comprehensive. The book assumes no prior dramatic training or experience with adolescents.

This book *does* assume that what drama coaches and group leaders need most (besides good scripts) are specific drama activities that will appeal to adolescent actors. These activities should help to free the performer's creativity and to develop technical skills on stage. The activities should lend themselves, if need be, to dramatizing ideas — say those in Scouting, an English book or a discussion group. In addition, these projects should not tax available space, supplies or noise tolerance.

In this book are approximately 50 such activities — enough for a semester-long drama course, a summer of dramatics or a year of once-a-week sessions.

This book is divided into five sections. The first chapter, "Terms and Goals for Performers," defines basic theatre vocabulary and discusses goals actors should strive for in each performance. The second chapter, "Planning Your Program," offers suggestions for building a dramatics program and provides tips for organizing and governing junior high-aged performers. Naturally, all group leaders eventually develop their own structure, rules and "theory" to suit their needs.

The final three chapters consist of the activities themselves, and focus on three major areas of drama: pantomime, voice and improvisation. Except for the poems and tongue-twisters recommended for practice, no scripts are necessary — all plots and dialogue emerge from the actors' imaginations.

In each chapter, the activities are prefaced by a brief introduction and divided into two groups: "short-short" impromptu activities, and longer, rehearsed performances. The "short-short" activities require no rehearsal and may be used as exercises to warm up, as activities to fill the last minutes of a session or as a project for the entire session.

The prepared performances require 10 to 90 minutes of rehearsal. Each activity is described in detail, including an example of the performance, recommended stage materials and time lengths, and suggestions for conducting the activity. Occasionally, the activities require some advance preparation by the leader or performer; these instances are marked with the notation "advanced preparation" and an asterisk. Each rehearsed performance also includes a worksheet (filled out as an example) that actors complete before rehearsing. Session leaders can omit or modify the written work according to their goals.

In general, the activities are arranged from the most simple to the most difficult. However, they need not be done in sequence, or with equal emphasis. An English teacher who wishes to incorporate dramatics into the classroom may want to work with poetry reading; a Scout leader wanting to put together a show of original work may want to focus largely on improvisation.

Adolescent actors are full of energy, emotion and curiosity about the theatre. They are eager to perform and to improve. I hope these ideas and activities will prove a stimulating, helpful resource for your group of young actors.

— Maria Novelly

CHAPTER I
TERMS & GOALS FOR PERFORMERS

INTRODUCTION

Whether the group members see themselves as future stars or just participate as a hobby, using common theatre vocabulary and setting standards for performance make each session more satisfying. These terms and standards need not be introduced at once, but can be discovered through the activities themselves. Pantomime activities lead naturally to emphasis on visibility, and voice activities lead to the standards for a satisfactory stage voice.

Listed below are basic stage terms and performance goals.

STAGE TERMS

1. **actor, performer:** *The "real person" on the stage.*

2. **actor positions:** *Terms that describe how directly the actor is facing the audience, as shown following:*

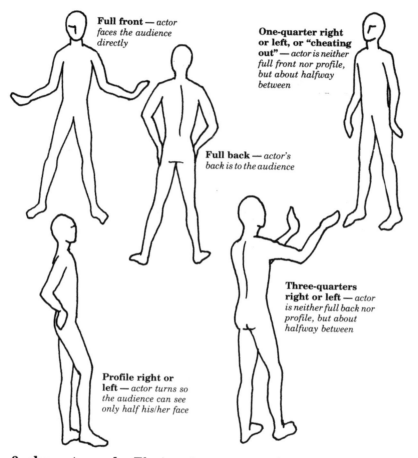

Full front — *actor faces the audience directly*

One-quarter right or left, or "cheating out" — *actor is neither full front nor profile, but about halfway between*

Full back — *actor's back is to the audience*

Three-quarters right or left — *actor is neither full back nor profile, but about halfway between*

Profile right or left — *actor turns so the audience can see only half his/her face*

3. **character, role:** *The imaginary person, thing or animal the actor pretends to be on stage.*

4. **cue:** *A signal to begin action or dialogue.*

5. **dialogue:** *Spoken words on stage.*

6. **downstage:** *A movement or area **toward** the audience.*

7. **duet scene:** *A scene for two people.*

8. **exposition:** *Information given through dialogue during a scene that explains events leading up to the action.*

9. **gesture:** *A movement, usually of the arm, that helps to express an idea or feeling.*

10. **hand prop:** *a prop that can be easily handled. Examples include books, chalk, dishes, baseball bats. In pantomime, hand props are usually imaginary.*

11. **improvisation:** (often abbreviated *improv*) *A scene performed with little or no rehearsal; it usually includes dialogue.*

12. **monologue, solo scene:** *A scene for one actor, who speaks his or her thoughts aloud or talks to an imaginary character or directly to the audience.*

13. **pantomime:** *A performance that communicates an idea or an action without using dialogue.*

14. **set:** *The actual pieces of furniture, platforms or other items (or their lack) on the stage.*

15. **set prop:** *A large prop, such as a piece of furniture, that is not easily moved. Examples include chairs, tables, fireplaces, platforms. In pantomimes, set props like chairs are usually real; all others are imaginary.*

16. **setting:** *The imaginary place and time the stage area represents.*

17. **sight cue:** *A visual signal for actors to begin action or dialogue, or for the audience to quiet down for a performance.*

18. **stage areas:** *For convenience, the acting area is divided into nine areas, as show below.*

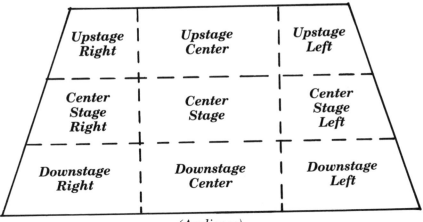

(Audience)

19. **stage left:** *A movement or area on the actor's left as he or she faces the audience.*

20. **stage property:** (usually abbreviated *prop*) *Any item used on stage.*

21. stage right: *A movement or area on the actor's right as he or she faces the audience.*

22. upstage: *A movement or area **away** from the audience.*

PERFORMANCE GOALS

1. **visibility:** If actors hope to communicate ideas to their audience, their bodies and faces must be seen; they must be visible. These techniques help:

   a. **hair:** Keep long bangs and hair out of eyes.

   b. **face and body:** Position these toward the audience as much as possible. In pantomimes, imaginary props can be placed between the performers and audience; real props can be placed to the side of the actors.

   c. **Cheat out,** or *open up,* as much as possible. Certainly, in real life, two people would face each other directly across a table, or they would cluster in a circle. On the stage, however, the table chairs would be angled out toward the audience, and the group would form a semi-circle or stand in an angled line. On stage, actors should try to use one-quarter positions instead of profile or three-quarter positions.

d. gestures: Use the arm farthest from the audience (upstage arm) for gestures or reaching. If you kneel on one knee, kneel on the upstage knee.

Wrong   ***Right***

e. turns: When you turn, turn so you face the audience during your turn.

f. crossing stage: When two or more actors cross the stage, the actor closest to the audience (downstage actor) should slightly trail the other actor, so as not to block that actor, as shown below.

2. **energy and absorption:** Performers must attend to the imaginary events on stage, and block out off-stage distractions. Most adolescents know what it is like to become so involved in a game, a TV show, a conversation with their friends or a book, that they honestly do not hear their parents or teachers talking to them. The performers must bring the same degree of energetic, unshakable involvement to the imaginary events on stage. If the actors are caught up and interested in the on-stage action, the audience will be, too.

3. **energy and expression:** The same energy that allows performers to absorb themselves in the stage action should also add power to their vocal and physical expressiveness. In real life, gestures, facial expressions and vocal tones are often subtle and monotonous. Not so on the stage. The entire body should be emotionally involved. The stage is no place for performers to be chewing gum, staring off over the audience or standing with crossed ankles.

   a. **gestures:** These involve the entire arm, not just the hand or forearm. Actors should feel as if the gesture originated from their very middle (waistline, bellybutton). Gestures should start definitely, end definitely and, for a fraction of a second after their completion, be held.

   b. **facial expressions:** These should be bigger and bolder than in real life. Like gestures, they can be held a bit.

4. **length:** Actors usually need minimum and maximum time lengths for their scenes. If a scene has been too short, elicit discussion about incidents that could have been included to make the scene fulfill the time limits. Point out to the actors that most radio and TV shows have strict time limits, and as beginners in the field, they should learn to automatically attend to the required scene length.

5. **exploitation:** This word has negative connotations, but it applies to the creativity of the performers: do they *exploit* the given situation or initial idea for all of its possible outcomes and developments?

CHAPTER II

PLANNING
YOUR
PROGRAM

INTRODUCTION

In order to help your young performers best develop their acting skills, you'll need to be prepared with plans regarding the time period allotted to the class; the working space your group will have; available materials; the manner in which you'll handle group work and scene presentations; that all-important first session; and the reasons your group is studying drama.

In the sections which follow, I have provided you with some plans of attack in these areas. I've found young students work best in an organized atmosphere.

TIME

The first thing you need to know or decide is the number and length of the session you will conduct. Is your dramatics program a semester-long course that meets every day for 45 minutes? Is it three two-hour, once-a-week, after-school meetings with a Scout troop? Is it a weekend workshop consisting of sessions Saturday and Sunday mornings and afternoons? Each option presents its own advantages and inconveniences.

GROUPS THAT MEET OCCASIONALLY

For groups that meet infrequently for a lengthy session (more than one hour), try to make each session self-contained. Forgetfulness and absenteeism can wreak havoc with work in progress. Begin each session with a series of group warm-up exercises, chosen from the impromptu group pantomimes or vocal warm-up sections in Chapters III and IV of this book. Then have two to four possible rehearsed scenes in mind to assign. Be prepared with a variety — it's hard for young actors, especially after a day of school, to do all pantomime.

After the warm-ups, assign one of the rehearsed scenes; allow rehearsal time, and then have those scenes presented. Then, as a break from rehearsing, try one of the solo impromptu exercises, or work on a directed poetry reading. As time permits, assign a second rehearsed scene, and end the sessions with those performances.

GROUPS THAT MEET FREQUENTLY (4-5 TIMES A WEEK)

If your group meets several times a week, you will gain in continuity. If the sessions are short, however, having enough time to rehearse and perform the rehearsed scenes is impossible in many instances. For adequate rehearsal time, shorten or eliminate the warm-up exercises. Furthermore, the performers should have an opportunity to "re-rehearse" their scenes if a day lapses between the first preparation time and the performance time. Again, absenteeism can present problems. For example, three scenes are ready for Wednesday, but the bell rings; on the following day, all three scenes are missing actors. In these cases, it is usually better to ask someone to step in and substitute for an actor than let the scene disintegrate over the course of time.

A group that meets frequently for short sessions over a long period of time can approach the activities more slowly and work on the techniques of pantomime, speech and improvisation more thoroughly. Work to be prepared at home, such as the solo pantomimes and monologues, can be assigned and critiqued.

Here is a possible syllabus for an 18-week course:

4-5 weeks	Pantomime activities, concluding with solo pantomime to music
4-5 weeks	Voice activities, concluding with self-directed poetry readings
9 weeks	Improvisation, concluding with monologue

WEEKEND WORKSHOPS

Weekend workshops call for a great variety of activities. Begin with plenty of warm-ups and exercises involving the entire group, such as the relaxation and imaginative journey exercises in the pantomime section. Then assign some group scenes, some in pantomime and some as improvised scenes. If the group is largely of beginners, emphasize techniques of visibility and introduce a few stage terms. If you want to work with prepared solo scenes, assign them to be performed the second day, when the participants are feeling more at ease with each other. After lunch breaks, always begin again with a short set of physical and vocal warm-ups.

SPACE

In planning your program, a second consideration is available space. A fairly isolated large room, such as a school cafeteria, is ideal. When actors work on group scenes, groups can spread out and rehearse without disturbing each other, and yet you can supervise the entire group and coach individual groups as necessary. If the room has a raised stage, a couple of groups can share it for rehearsal, and all groups can perform on it. The stage is also the best place for warm-up activities. If the room has no raised stage, choose a meeting area for warm-ups and performances. For the sake of variety, change this meeting area from time to time.

Usually, such ideal conditions do not prevail. More likely, you will be working in a small room, bounded by math classes or committee meetings whose participants do not appreciate the sounds of rehearsal or warm-up chants. In such cases, try to clear an area suitable for warm-ups, even if the actors must move chairs and desks each session. For warm-ups, actors should be able to stretch their arms out to each side and to the front and back without hitting anyone else.

Group rehearsals will prove most frustrating. Sending a few well-behaved groups outside the room may be possible if no one else is disturbed; even so, stand in the doorway so you can easily monitor all groups. If sending groups outside the room is impossible, select, as often as possible, activities that take minimum rehearsal and performance space — the voice activities and all the short-short activities require little or no rehearsal space. For the rehearsed improvisations and pantomimes, you can simply shorten the preparation time and have each group plan its action and rehearse minimally. Even the sketchiest rehearsal in a classroom aisle is more beneficial than a long, argumentative discussion.

MATERIALS

A third consideration is that of materials. A few items are essential; many others are simply nice to have.

CHAIRS

Sturdy chairs are absolutely necessary; non-folding chairs are better than folding chairs, but the latter are adequate for most scenes. Chairs can be placed side by side to make a couch or bed; they can become thrones or subway seats with just a turn of the imagination. Usually, a scene will call for no more than six chairs. However, if several groups are rehearsing simultaneously, each group will need a set of chairs. If you only have a few, allow each group to have one or two, and tell the actors that they must imagine the others during rehearsal, but that they can use real chairs for performance.

TABLE

A second essential set prop is a table. A couple of small tables, such as elementary school desks, are extremely useful. Two can be used as a dining table; individually, such tables can be used as end tables, office desks, kitchen and bank counters, etc. Again, if you do not have enough tables for group rehearsals, have the actors imagine them until the actual performance.

ADDITIONAL PROPS

For pantomime and voice activities, the above set props are sufficient. For the improvisations, however, additional hand props can increase interest and creativity. Sturdy items such as plastic dishes, pans and coffeepots, plastic flowers, flatware, plastic bottles, milk cartons and other boxes of various sizes, an old suitcase and a telephone are invaluable. The participants can donate these items if they have them at home, or you can purchase them at thrift shops and rummage sales. Avoid borrowing items; stage use is wearing for props.

COSTUMES

In addition, a set of costumes for impromptu use is helpful and popular with the actors. The most useful items are grey-haired wigs, aprons, long dresses, suit jackets, shawls, oddly-shaped eyeglasses, scarves, ties and hats. Again, donated or thrift-shop items are the best. When you get to the group scenes, actors may bemoan the fact that only one long blue dress is available; however, there is nothing wrong with everyone sharing the same long blue dress. But used frequently, costumes soil quickly. Try to send everyone home with a plastic bag full of costumes so you don't end up doing all the laundry yourself.

STORAGE

If you use materials, you must also have a storage area, even if it is just a set of large cardboard boxes. Obviously, available storage will limit your prop selection. Label storage areas clearly and always allow enough time at the end of each session for the actors to return materials to their proper places. Adolescents tend to be irresponsible unless you prod them along.

In addition, formulate a few rules for prop use. Fragile props such as telephones can be reserved for "performance only," and *all* props are for rehearsal use only — *not* for pre-session baseball practice.

SUPPLIES
In addition, useful supplies include a pair of scissors, tape, paper, markers, string and, above all, safety pins. If your program budget allows, you can supply items like markers and construction paper — and expect to make constant purchases of safety pins. If cash is in short supply, however, omit activities such as announcing pantomimes with the use of signs, and have the actors give the title of their scene orally, or ask the actors to bring their own signs.

DISAPPEARING ITEMS
Young, excited performers may borrow props, supplies or costumes and forget to return them at the end of the session. A practical solution: have each user give you some "collateral" for the use of the items. The user gives you a key or a wallet, or book, or jacket, and gets the needed item; after the user is finished, all items are returned to the original parties.

Naturally, your budget, storage space and scrounging energies pose the only limits to how many stage materials your program can handle. Phone ringers, platforms, couches and camp cots are all nice to have. Performance, as opposed to design, however, intensely interests most beginning actors, so you may want to distribute your own energies accordingly.

GROUP WORK
In assigning group scenes, I urge that you avoid having the same groups work together each time. From the first day, make it your prerogative to place people randomly into groups, and continue to do so throughout the sessions. Occasionally, let them choose their partners (especially in duets), but all in all, having assigned, rotating groups reduces friction among the inevitable cliques and lessens the chance of hurt feelings. Point out that: (1) in professional theatre, indeed in all of adult life, people work with others who are not their bosom buddies; (2) these groups are not lifelong marriages, just 20- to 40-minute acting projects, and surely anyone can survive that!; and (3) even people that one may not cultivate as friends have good ideas and unique talents that can contribute to a scene and one's growth as an actor. These arguments stave off grumbling and build a positive attitude, although you may still have to confer privately with extremely immature actors.

For group work, actors tend to be more organized and productive if they do the written worksheet. Many of the worksheet samples include a "background" section in which they interview each other and share experiences and opinions — simply a device to help them get acquainted.

Each worksheet sample contains similar elements. In an "idea" section, actors record a number of ideas for a scene, one of which they choose. Similar to brainstorming, this process helps the actors to open up to possibilities, instead of grasping the first — and often least original — idea that occurs to them. Often, even with a list of four or five good possible ideas, a group's members will wail, "We can't think of anything." In these cases, glance at their list, which probably contains at least three good possibilities, and tell them to try out at least two ideas before they decide nothing will work. If they declare that they cannot think of *any* ideas, demand that they write down *any* idea that occurs to them.

Too often, group members will get critical before they get creative. In these cases, tell them they can't create and criticize at the same time. For the best scene, the group must first create (simply put down ideas) and *then* criticize (choose, add, delete, arrange, try out) and develop their ideas.

Finally, in some instances, different groups will come up with the same idea. Once discovered, this situation can upset everyone; simply point out that by definition, different people will present the same ideas in different ways. Despite their worries, the actors have no problems.

Once the actors choose their scene idea, they record ideas for developing the scene — possible complications, outcomes, interesting details. This process helps the actors to "exploit" their initial situation. Finally, the actors summarize the planned stage action in complete sentences, and note other production information, such as hand props, scene title, etc.

In using the written work, you can either mimeograph sheets with the main (capitalized) headings on them and leave spaces for the actors to fill in their ideas, or you can write the headings on the board and have the actors recopy them on their own paper. I prefer the second method. Since the actors must recopy everything, they also read it more carefully and will spontaneously ask questions if they don't understand.

Once the groups are formed and the activity is explained, the actors complete and turn in their written work — if they are doing it — *before* they begin to rehearse. Encourage the actors to sit in a circle and discuss their ideas as they plan their scene. Each group should have a specific, assigned rehearsal area and each group must respect the boundaries of other rehearsal areas. If the actors are using props, they should first rehearse without props a couple of times, and then with props. As the groups rehearse, circulate among them, coaching as appropriate.

As the actors complete their rehearsals, they sign up for performance order. Keep a firm grip on this list. If you simply post it, actors have too much fun crossing out and rearranging names! Actors perform in the order that they sign up (requests of "second" or "fifth" should not be honored), and they should not sign up if they feel unprepared to perform right then. Of course, some groups will always be eager to perform; others will hang back, professing they don't want to; and each group will need a different amount of rehearsal time. Those who finish first can polish their scenes, practice their introductions, develop a second scene, or visit with each other. These "early birds" should avoid disturbing other groups still in rehearsal. Once two-thirds of the groups have signed up, announce a limit on the remaining rehearsal time, complete the list, and begin the performances.

SCENE PRESENTATION

Performances presented during each session are more orderly and enjoyable if the participants use a standard procedure for getting the audience's attention, presenting pertinent information, and beginning and ending the scene. Stress the importance of introducing scenes concisely, self-confidently and clearly.

The following procedure works well:

1. **set-up:** The performers set up their stage, placing props.

2. **sight cue:** The performers line up in a row downstage (near the audience). This is a "sight cue," or visual signal for the audience to settle down and pay attention.

3. **introduction:** The performers introduce the scene by announcing a title and any other information necessary to understand the scene. Performers avoid elaborate explanations of floorplans or previous action; the title does not give away the scene's outcome. For the first-day pantomime on page 15, the performers need only say, "This is our group pantomime." In beginning sessions, or before unfamiliar audiences, the performers can also give their names.

4. **position and action:** The actors then silently take their positions on stage, freeze briefly and begin the scene. After the scene is played, actors still on stage freeze again, relax, and drop their heads. At the close of polished scenes, actors can again line up downstage for a bow.

5. **clean-up:** If the actors have used props or costumes in their scene, they return them immediately to their proper storage areas.

In the introductions to the first scenes performed, you may find that actors tend to mumble, look at the floor and stand with their legs crossed. In such cases, you can assign the following introduction scene.

Introduction Scene #1

Performance: Working in groups of four to five, performers introduce an invisible scene.

Example: Performers line up on stage, wait for the audience to quiet down, and give an introduction. One performer says simply: "This is our invisible scene," and then each actor gives his or her name.

Preparation time: two to five minutes

Performance time: 30 seconds

Stage materials: none

Suggestions for conducting the activity: Give the above example, and quickly assign the actors into groups. Ask them what every scene needs to have at its beginning. Explain that an introduction provides the audience its first impression of an actor, and helps the audience prepare for the scene to follow.

Actors should make a clear, confident introduction an automatic part of every scene; therefore, they must practice the introduction alone, without having to think about a following scene. Since their scene is invisible in this instance, they have no need to act it out.

During an introduction, actors should establish eye contact with the audience, stand with their weight on both feet, and speak with clear, loud voices. Titles and names in particular should be emphasized, not slurred over.

If the introduction is sloppy, interrupt and ask the actors to repeat it. You may need to demonstrate clear speech; for example, say: "This is our iNVisiBLe SCeNe," hitting all consonants hard.

Introduction Scene #2

Performance: Working in groups of five, actors give an introduction to an invisible scene that has a title, characters and some important previous action. Performers may use scenes from books, movies or TV shows as material.

Example: Actors line up downstage. One begins by saying, "This is our invisible Robin Hood scene." Another says, "This scene takes place in the woods, and Friar Tuck (at which point another actor chimes in: "played by me, Sam Sammuelson,") has just arrived with news from the castle." The other actors then say: "I play Robin Hood," "I play Maid Marian," "I play King John," and "I play his henchman."

Preparation time: 10 minutes

Performance time: one minute

Stage materials: none

Suggestions for conducting the activity: Again, stress the importance of clear, concise, helpful introductions.

Advance preparation: Ask the performers to listen carefully to introductions given to acts in variety shows and for guests on talk shows. Ask them to collect ideas about how to interest the audience in what follows.

THE FIRST DAY

For the first session with a new group of inexperienced actors, the following discussion activity works well.

Drama Discussion Exercise

1. Ask the group the question, "What is drama?" Give them some time to think, and try to elicit at least one response from each participant. Tell the group you intend to get a number of responses that equals the number of people in the room. To get a large number of responses, you may have to prod: "We have only 18! We need three more!"

2. Record all answers, no matter how tangential or unrelated, on a board or large sheet of paper. Try to avoid expression of strong approval or disapproval, and try to remain as neutral for the inevitable responses of "sex" and "gunfights" as for those of "costumes" and "scripts."

3. After you have recorded an appropriate number of responses, step back, look at the board or paper, and observe that drama is a wide field, as your group has shown. Then circle the word *acting*, which is bound to have cropped up, and announce that the main purpose of the sessions is for the participants to develop their acting skills.

   This brief discussion reassures most of the group because their main purpose in attending the sessions *is* to learn acting. At the same time, it relieves the odd few who honestly want to stay off the stage, either out of sheer terror or studied disinterest; this exercise helps them see that drama involves many other skills.

4. Then, changing the subject, ask if anyone has looked at *The Book of Lists* and seen the list of things "people are most afraid of." Ask those who have seen the list to please keep quiet, and then ask the others to guess what people are most afraid of. After some discussion, someone will guess or reveal that people are most afraid of "being in front of other people." Then tell them that they are doing something most people would find very frightening; it's natural and expected that beginning actors feel somewhat anxious. Such nervousness need not, of course, be a harbinger of failure.

First-Day Pantomime

Performance: Working in groups of five to seven, actors pantomime a single general activity, supplied on a card by the session leader. In order to communicate the idea of a *general* activity, each actor in the group must pantomime a related *specific* activity. The audience then guesses the general activity and each specific activity. As soon as an actor's specific activity is guessed, he or she may stop and stand still until the audience guesses all activities. The actors need *not* interact with each other on stage.

Example: Six actors pantomime the general activity of "basic training" by pantomiming the following specific activities: shooting a rifle, doing jumping jacks, climbing a rope, saluting, crawling under a fence, polishing boots. The audience will usually first recognize the general activity and then point out the different specific activities.

Preparation time: five minutes

Performance time: (per group) one to two minutes

Stage materials: chairs

*Advance preparation: Group leader should put the different general activities (see list at end of this section) on index cards or slips of paper.

Suggestions for conducting the activity: Quickly assign participants into groups and hand each group a card with a general activity written on it. Make sure that all actors know they are to *pantomime* an activity, and not to speak.

As the participants plan their performances, circulate around the room, making sure that each group member plans to do a *different* specific activity. Be prepared to prod: "What are some things you do when you build a house?" Keep the planning time short — five minutes should suffice.

This activity makes an excellent beginning event. The participants are usually excited to be on stage the very first day. They get to act without having to plan extensively; the scene requirements are easy; and they find comfort in not having to go on stage alone.

Suggested General Activities:

- housework
- playing (different) sports at school
- gardening
- camping
- office work
- hospital work
- building a house

- time at the beach

- circus acts

- performing with an orchestra or band

FOR THE CLASSROOM TEACHER

If you teach a drama class, as opposed to coaching drama after school, you will find that students often expect drama to be a "goof-off" or recess period. In the long run, it helps to conduct the first few sessions in a serious, business-like fashion.

I usually assign students to a seating arrangement within the first five minutes of the first session. Whether you use alphabetical seating or allow the students to stay where they choose, a permanent seating chart increases classroom order.

Second, take a few minutes to go over classroom policies. Copies of rules concerning late work, use of materials, etc., can be handed out for the students to keep. Having the students take them home to be signed by their parents can ward off future misunderstandings.

After these stern matters, you are ready to launch into the discussion and pantomime activities outlined earlier in this chapter.

FOR SCOUT, RECREATIONAL AND CHURCH ACTIVITY LEADERS

Whether the goal of your program is simply to foster good times and friendships, or to build a full-scale dramatics program, this book provides a wide choice of appropriate materials. If your goal is largely discussion and learning, in the classroom or church group, refer also to the next section, "Adapting Activities for Discussion and Learning." The index to activities, which classifies them as "easy," "most advanced," "adaptable for church discussion use," etc., also provides help in choosing activities.

If your program already has a slot for drama, great! Simply experiment with a mix of activities that best fit your time limitations and the interests of your group. If you do meet infrequently (weekly, biweekly or monthly), try to begin each session with an exercise in which you lead the entire group (vocal warm-ups and imaginative journeys are good). For each session, have in mind more activities than you think you'll need; it's hard to accurately predict how long completion of an activity will take.

Perhaps your main objective is to provide a range of activities, drama among them. Perhaps you are uncertain about how large a part drama will play in your program, but you'd like to experiment. In these cases, go easy on trying to develop acting techniques and concentrate on activities that are simple and entertaining. You may choose to eliminate references to "drama" altogether, and refer to the exercises as games, activities or something new to try. Characters and stars from TV shows and movies are popular with young teens, and it's easy to get a group interested in acting.

For an introductory or one-time session, keep things simple and define "acting" as pretending something and communicating what is being pretended. The group can provide lots of examples from the media. Start with the "First-Day Pantomime" (page 15). The "Walking Through" impromptu pantomime (page 29) helps loosen up imaginations, as do the relaxation and imaginative journey exercises (pages 31-35). Move on and try some vocal exercises, such as "Color Your Words" and "Greeting by Number" (pages 66-68). Let the group experiment with improvisation. Do a round of "Add-on Story" (page 91), and let them try their hand at "Group Improvs with a Given Situation" (pages 94-96), perhaps making a few prefacing remarks about scene-building (pages 90-91). The "Who Began" or "Selling" games are fun conclusions (pages 37 and 36). Of course, this first session can be shortened easily by deleting activities.

As group interest and time warrants, you can easily expand from this introductory, yet self-contained, session. If the group chooses to devote more time to dramatics and moves into rehearsed scenes, the written work can be shortened or omitted, although the "idea sheet" portion of each activity seems to produce more creative scenes and more orderly rehearsals. If the sessions are fairly long (more than an hour) and your group is small, it is vital to provide variety and lively pace; left to sit around and think and discuss too much, self-conscious adolescents may think themselves out of performing without the pressure of a grade.

ADAPTING ACTIVITIES
FOR DISCUSSION AND LEARNING

Perhaps your program focuses on learning or discussing issues in a church or classroom setting. To spark discussion or reinforce learning in church youth groups, English or social studies classes, many activities in this book can be adapted with little alteration. The index to activities gives a concise listing of the most obvious choices. This section turns attention to the particular needs of the social studies teacher, the English teacher and the church youth activity director.

SOCIAL STUDIES

The history or geography class could adapt the "Walking Through" impromptu group pantomimes (page 29) as a fun, end-of-class-period review:

- "Walk like you're invading the D-Day beaches!"

- "Walk through the Everglades!"

- "Walk like fugitives escaping north!"

- "Walk though Antarctica!"

Responses may be stereotypic, but reinforcing and "right-brained." Interview scenes (page 82) of famous figures are excellent ways of presenting biographical material. Emphasize that the interviewer should concentrate on the memorable and interesting events or accomplishments, not just a series of dates. Instead of producing "Commercials for Products That Don't Exist" (pages 124-125), produce commercials for products of a particular area or country, such as products from Brazil or the Midwest in the United States. Historical inventions and discoveries are also good subjects for commercials:

- Galileo demonstrates the telescope.

- Early people point out the advantages of fire.

- A satisfied 19th century traveler raves about the steam engine.

News broadcasts need not be low-voiced (page 80), but can recount important historical events, such as exploration in the 16th century or milestones in the building of civil rights for blacks. Lastly, the one situation-three ways scene can be expanded and adapted: the outbreak of the American Civil War would bring different reactions from Abraham Lincoln, Robert E. Lee, a Northerner, a Southerner and a slave.

ENGLISH

For the English classroom, the voice exercises are appropriate. "Color Your Words" (page 66) provides practice with connotation, and directed poetry readings create interest in that form of literature. Descriptive, dramatic prose passages could also undergo directed, expressive readings. Interview scenes (page 82) can focus on literary characters or authors, and the advice column scenes (pages 70 and 75) offer good practice in proper letter-writing form and punctuation of quotations.

CHURCH YOUTH ACTIVITIES

Dramatics in youth group activities can be used for two purposes — to promote friendship and fellowship or to illustrate an idea or spark discussion. Planning dramatic activities for the first purpose is covered in the section, "For Scout, Recreational and Church Activity Leaders." For the second purpose, many activities in this book are easily adapted and incorporated into a discussion or a lesson.

Youth groups often focus on open discussion of teen concerns. Four activities that make good discussion-starters are adaptations of "Advice Column Scene #1" (page 70), the "If-I-Had-It-My-Way Scene" (page 107), "Commercials for Products That Don't Exist" (pages 124-125) and "One Situation-Three Attitudes Scene" (page 128). Used correctly, these activities can be done very seriously, although the sample performances in this book highlight the activities' entertaining and actor-training side.

In using the "Advice Column Scene," ask each letter-writer to describe a serious, real-life problem that he or she knows someone is facing — perhaps one similar to those the group has been discussing. For example, the relationship between the parents is deteriorating, or a friend is getting deeper into drugs. In turn, each advisor gives a thoughtful answer, based on biblical example, or ethical choices, or good communication practices, or whatever the group is currently working on. As a whole, the group can discuss the problems and answers.

The "If-I-Had-It-My-Way Scene" can take the title of "If Christianity Had Its Way" or "If People Acted in Sharing and Caring Ways." Communication situations are obvious subjects for these scenes: Scene 1 shows a mother and daughter shopping together, disagreeing about what outfit to buy. Tempers flare; blame, resentment and hurt are shown. Scene 2 still portrays the two in disagreement, but in a spirit of openness and compromise and willingness to listen, with the daughter leading the way.

Larger themes of poverty, racism and war also could be explored in this way. How could an international conflict or the specter of millions starving be handled in a truly Christian or caring, loving way? How is it usually handled? How a teen-ager can live with the way it is usually handled might be the real meat of the discussion that follows these scenes.

Young teen-agers usually have strong feelings about situations they have found unfair, wrong or badly handled; they have also usually been in situations in which they wished they had acted differently. By participating in scenes that depict situations as they would *like* to see them unfold in life, they gain confidence that they can help change attitudes and behavior in their lives.

"Commercials for Products That Don't Exist" are easily adapted as commercials for love, listening, fairness, self-esteem, peace, brotherhood, generosity and other themes you may be exploring with your group. What are the advantages and benefits of withstanding peer pressure? How is life made easier and happier by trying to listen to one's parents before deciding they hate their children by imposing so many rules? "How-to" commercials are an excellent format — how to show you're a Christian in school or at a dance; how to see yourself as a success in God's eyes even if you seem a failure by external standards (D's on report card, didn't make track team).

A final discussion-starting activity is the "One Situation-Three Attitudes Scene," which can be transformed into a "one conflict-three attitudes scene." This conflict can be external or internal. For example, a scene may show a young teen-ager being asked to drive a car even though he/she has no license. One person plays the teen-ager, and another plays a person egging him or her on. Four other people could voice the opposing voices (viewpoints) in the teen-ager's mind:

- say *yes*, and never mind the consequences?

- say *yes*, and feel nervous and pressured?

- say *no*, and feel left-out and "wimpy?"

- say *no*, and somehow retain the respect of the other?

As a whole, the group could discuss the various choices facing this teen-ager.

The activities described above lend themselves to use as effective and lively discussion-starters. However, youth activity program participants also study biblical literature and religious themes in formal ways. Voice exercises and directed poetry reading (pages 64-66 and 68-69) can be used with psalms, descriptive passages and some of the more exciting stories.

Interview scenes, of course, lend themselves to study of biblical characters or important figures in church history. An interesting twist is to have creatures from outer space interview earthlings about their beliefs. Finally, reading parables aloud and recreating them with modern applications helps to integrate scripture message into today's culture. The parables of the prodigal son, pearl of great price, the good Samaritan and many of those found in Luke and Matthew are excellent. For example, group members can study the parable of the good Samaritan, brainstorm analogous modern situations, and act them out.

CHAPTER III
PANTOMIME

INTRODUCTION

Of all the facets of professional theatre, pantomime ranks as the most difficult, time-consuming and technically complicated. Yet this drama book, like many drama texts, begins with pantomime. Why? Not to turn beginning actors into miniature Marcel Marceaus, but to give them a means to develop confidence and stage skills. Visibility, gesture, expression, absorption and energy are paramount in pantomime, and beginning actors can concentrate fully on these qualities, unburdened by concern over dialogue, projection and use of hand props.

Communicating an idea and practicing stage skills, rather than precise miming, form the emphasis of these activities. Although you can demonstrate mime techniques (stair-climbing, rope-pulling, etc.), training actors in mime techniques is almost impossible unless you work with a small, dedicated and talented group.

BASIC QUALITIES OF GOOD PANTOMIME

Even without much training or time, you can emphasize three qualities necessary to effective pantomime:

1. **consistency:** Objects that are mimed must remain the same size. A steering wheel cannot shrink and expand; drinking glasses cannot float off in mid-air, but must be set down; a broom handle is not a wet noodle.

2. **exaggerated resistance:** If a mime pushes against a door, pulls a rope, lifts a suitcase, pushes a button, picks a flower, knocks on a door, lifts a weight, tightens a bolt, sews on a button or performs almost any action, the resistance of person against object *must* be exaggerated and made "bigger" than in real life. In real life, picking flowers may take no effort at all, but in pantomime, the actor must make the action more definite, sharper, bigger.

3. **exaggerated expression and gesture:** If a mime points to someone, cries, laughs, becomes sad or angry, reacts in shock or horror or joy, the facial expressions and gestures used must be exaggerated, or made bigger, than in real life.

BASICS OF PANTOMIME STORY LINES

In addition to mime techniques, original pantomimes must eventually — though not in the beginning exercises — tell a story and hold audience interest. The introduction to the chapter on improvisation covers methods of story development more thoroughly, but here are some suggestions:

1. **Keep it simple.** In pantomime, the storyline must be simple if the audience is to understand. The process of watching a well-executed pantomime is itself satisfying; a complicated plot simply muddies the action.

2. **Tell a story.** In making up a storyline, actors think in terms of an initial situation (beginning), complications and problems arising from that situation (middle), and a solution to those problems (ending).

3. **Be fantastic!** In pantomime, complications and solutions can be less realistic, more creative and more fantastic than those in realistic improvisations with dialogue. It's easy and entertaining to present, through mime, a shoe store scene in which the shoes are first too tight, then too loose, then too high, then too heavy, then just right but too expensive, with the customer finally deciding to go barefoot. (This situation is, of course, an exception to the rule of object consistency in pantomime.)

An interesting scene can develop from almost any initial situation, depending on the creativity of the actors. Such creativity, of course, is not universally distributed. Through repeated exercises and the use of the idea sheets, however, all group members develop and strengthen their creative skills.

SHORT-SHORT PANTOMIME ACTIVITIES

IMPROMPTU SOLO PANTOMIMES

Simple Actions

Performance: With only a few minutes to plan, an actor pantomimes a simple activity and the audience guesses what it is. The audience *waits* until the performance is completed before guessing. The audience then recounts details of the performance. The actor can also simply announce the activity in advance, in which case the audience does not guess the scene, but evaluates how skillfully the actor communicated. Actors can think up their own activities, or you can give them suggestions.

*Advance preparation: Prepare index cards with one activity written on each.

Suggested activities:

- playing a baseball position
- searching for water in the desert
- walking a dog
- washing a dog
- sleepwalking
- wading in a cold stream
- writing a letter, sealing it, stamping it
- playing golf
- carrying several pieces of luggage
- cutting out a sewing pattern
- shooting a gun or rifle
- building a model
- changing a flat tire
- serving a meal
- brushing teeth
- playing tennis
- giving a traffic ticket
- driving a car
- painting a room
- washing dishes
- washing a car
- building a campfire
- skiing
- training a pet
- learning to swim
- planting a garden
- setting a table
- cooking something (food can be specified)

- paddling a canoe
- putting groceries away
- shopping and standing in line to pay
- surfing
- looking for a contact lens
- crumpling up newspapers and packing a box
- wrapping presents
- arranging flowers
- watering a garden

Believable Entrances

From the moment actors enter on stage, they portray specific characters. In each of these exercises, the performers make entrances as specific characters in specific situations. The performers strive to communicate the age, the occupation and the mood of the characters involved. The characters are absorbed in what has just happened offstage, and what they want to do onstage.

A brief discussion makes this exercise more effective. Let's say a student enters a classroom, knowing he or she must take a difficult test for which he or she is unprepared. These are some of the questions to which an actor playing that character must have answers:

- What, specifically, does the hallway look like?

- What, specifically, does the classroom look like?

- Where does the student look?

- What is the student thinking about?

- How relaxed or tense is the student?

- How does the student move?

These questions are all imagined, but vivid, nonetheless.

Performance: Actors are given entrance situations, or they invent their own. Most of these scenes are too complicated to be guessed at — each performer can announce a simple title, such as "Job Interview." Actors develop each situation as fully as possible, while keeping the scene a solo performance. These situations can also be used as beginnings of fully-developed group pantomimes or improvisations.

*Advance preparation: Put the situations on index cards for easier handling.

Suggestions for entrance pantomimes:

- At the end of an unsuccessful day, an encyclopedia salesperson, carrying a heavy suitcase of samples, gets out of the car for one last call.

- A doctor emerges from the X-ray room to inform a patient that he/she has an incurable disease.

- A presidential candidate arrives at a victory party after winning/ losing an election.

- A teen-ager comes off a plane to greet a good friend/boring relative.

- A young child enters the kitchen, looking for forbidden cookies.

- A housewife hangs up the phone after learning a bit of juicy gossip, and goes out into the yard to tell a neighbor.

- A teen-ager returns home from the dentist, after having three cavities filled.

- A hiker finally reaches the mountain summit after climbing all day.

- A parent enters a messy living room after a long day at work.

- A new student leaves the lunch line, alone, and looks for a place to sit in the cafeteria.

- An athlete enters his/her bedroom after three hours of grueling practice.

- A young person enters an office for a job interview.

- An elderly person enters a train compartment, looking for a lost wallet/a lost pair of gloves.

- An actor steps out of a limousine on Academy Awards night.

- A babysitter enters to check on sleeping children.

- A middle-aged person enters a log cabin during a snowstorm.

- A teacher enters a classroom where students are misbehaving.

- A teen-ager enters a crowded hall, looking for a friend who is bringing along a blind date for the teen-ager.

- A child enters a movie theatre during an exciting film.

- A teen-ager enters the living room where a parent sits reading his/her bad report card.

- A student enters the principal's office because of misdeeds.

- A child wakes on Christmas morning and goes to open presents.

- A burglar enters a house.

Emotions

Performance: In these short, unrehearsed pantomime sketches, actors convey a specific emotional state. Although emotions can be communicated abstractly, actors fare better if they imagine and pantomime a situation in which a particular emotion might be dominant.

Example: Instead of thinking about "sad" in a general way, actors imagine situations where sadness occurs — saying goodbye to friends, receiving a letter with some bad news, attending a funeral. The group can prepare for the activity by doing a group "idea sheet" orally. In what different situations might a person show anger or excitement or loneliness?

*Advance preparation: Put the emotions on cards.

Suggested emotions:

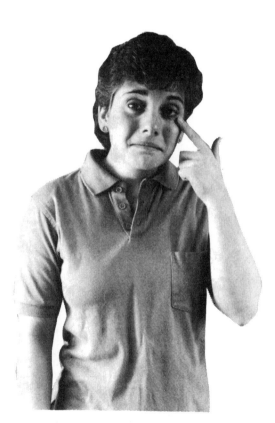

- cheerful
- energetic
- stubborn
- bossy
- impatient
- amused
- angry
- annoyed
- terrified
- lonely
- excited
- bored
- suspicious
- arrogant
- mischievous
- triumphant
- sly
- hesitant
- disgusted
- cold (or warm)
- indecisive
- exhausted
- tense
- friendly
- sulky
- sad

Walking Through

Performance: Divide the actors into groups of four to five members. Give each group a situation, preferably written on an index card, where people are "walking through" a particular setting. Each group has a few minutes to plan the action. The group members can announce the situation with a title beforehand, or the audience can guess *after* the actors have completed their scene. Don't forget to collect the cards!

*Advance preparation: Put the situations on index cards.

Suggested situations: Pretend you're walking . . .

- through tall under-brush.
- through a dark, danger-ous alley.
- across a wide street on a rainy, windy night.
- in the burning desert, looking for water.
- through a forest of man-eating plants.
- in outer space, weight-less.
- down a road of sticky asphalt and tar.
- across a log over a ravine full of crocodiles.
- across a street of broken glass.
- through a huge bowl of whipped cream.
- from the cold out-of-doors into a warm room.
- through a snowstorm.
- through a swamp.
- down a cold mountain stream.
- through a bowl of chewed-up bubble gum.
- across a room of bouncy springs.
- in a bowl of feathers.
- underwater.

MPTU GROUP PANTOMIMES

Join In

Performance: One participant goes up on stage and begins a simple activity. As audience members catch on, they raise their hands, and at a signal from the session leader, they go up, one at a time, and join in with the activity. No talking is allowed. In this exercise, technical skill is not as important as speedy communication and improvisation.

Depending on the size of the acting area, you may want to limit the final number of actors in the scene to six to 10. Caution the actors not to let the action devolve immediately into some form of combat; e.g., shoveling becomes a snowball fight, or flipping hotcakes becomes a free-for-all at the pancake house. Encourage actors to join the scene in a cooperative and helpful way and to ask themselves, before they raise their hands, "What can I do on stage that will help — not hinder — the activites already begun?" For practice, the group can write up an idea sheet. For example, if someone begins pantomiming painting something, what are a dozen logical, interesting, helpful activities that would add to the scene?

Example: The beginning activity is simple and easily recognizable. To pantomime making sandwiches, begin with bread and knife in hand, not by getting ingredients out of cabinets. However, expect some interesting results from misread cues: if an actor goes on stage and begins shoveling what he or she thinks is snow, unless he/she clearly communicates the idea of winter weather, the joiners may read the scene as being in a coal mine!

Ideas for beginnings:

- flipping pancakes
- sweeping the floor
- painting a wall
- typing
- sawing wood
- building a fire
- watering plants
- juggling
- playing in a rock band/ orchestra
- shoveling snow
- lifting weights
- fishing
- looking at scenery and taking pictures
- mixing a drink

Continuation Dream

Divide participants into groups of four. Assign each person within a group a number. Then ask the actors to think about dreams. Remind them that dreams are abstract, without plot, logic, and are often soundless or in slow motion. Settings change without warning, events take unexpected twists, and two or three unrelated actions might take place simultaneously.

Performance: Each group acts out a dream pantomime in which members may sing, make sound effects, or utter single words, but speak no dialogue.

Example: They develop the scene as follows. Person #1 goes on stage and begins any activity he or she chooses. At a signal from the group leader, #2 goes on stage — choosing to interact with the first performer or to do something totally unrelated. Then #3 enters on signal, followed by #4, each extending the dream in any manner he/she chooses. At the leader's signal, and in order, #1, #2 and #3 exit the stage, leaving #4 to end the dream.

Relaxation and Imaginative Journeys

If these activities are presented as serious, sophisticated exercises — which they are — young performers respond well. In an imaginative journey, the participants imagine, respond to, and act out appropriate actions as they listen to the leader describe the events of a "journey." Sometimes the actors interact with each other; at other times, they react individually. If you have enough space, the entire group can participate at the same time. The actors become more absorbed in this activity if you precede it with a relaxation exercise, which is conducted as follows:

Relaxation Exercise

Actors lie on the floor on their backs, with their arms at their sides, their legs uncrossed, and their eyes closed. Ask them to imagine that their entire bodies are very heavy, sinking to the floor.

Slowly mention different parts of the body, all of which are getting heavier and heavier: toes, ankles, wrists, fingernails, necks, heads, hair, eyelids. Ask them to imagine that they are lying on soft, warm sand on a sunny day. Ask them to imagine they are bathed in soft light, vorite color. Ask them to imagine they are surrounded by the sounds of the sea — waves washing against the shore, seagulls crying in the distance. Then the actors slowly rise, as they feel ready to do so, and open their eyes, remaining silent at all times. They can now go on an imaginative journey.

Imaginative Journey #1

After the actors have stood up, ask them to imagine and act out the following:

They walk away from the beach, over some sand dunes and through some tall grass. They then enter a dark forest, which stretches in all directions. After the warmth of the beach, the forest is cool and dark. The walkers realize that they no longer know their way, and they begin to hear strange noises, frightening noises, that come from all directions.

They search, more and more frantically, for recognizable landmarks. Then, through the increasing gloom, they spot another person (another actor) in the forest. They feel relieved to find each other, and tell each other, *in pantomime*, how they have become lost. They continue on together.

Meanwhile, the noises come closer and sound more dangerous; the night grows colder and more foreboding. Pairs of actors find other pairs; they exchange stories, *in pantomime*, and go on together as a foursome. They discover a huge rock cliff that rises high above them and to each side as far as they can see. One group member finds an opening under the cliff, large enough for one person to squeeze through. The group members help each other through the opening, and they find themselves back in warmth and sunlight.

Imaginative Journey #2

After the actors have stood up on the beach, ask them to imagine the following:

They see and feel the sun going behind the clouds; the wind begins to blow. The wind gets stronger and stronger, and rain begins to fall — at first only in isolated drops, but then in a cold, driving, wind-whipped downpour. They gather their beach belongings and rush for shelter in a small hut nearby. They enter and find wood to build a fire. As the fire begins to blaze, the actors warm themselves until they feel comfortable again. They look out a window and see the sun shining again. They go to open the door and find that they cannot get out! They push and pry at the door, but to no avail. Suddenly, they hear a piercing sound that hurts their ears. Then silence. They try the door again — still locked.

They look around and see another door, a very tiny door. They try this door, and it opens to reveal a narrow passageway. They hesitate; they hear the piercing sound again. They enter the passageway. It is dark and full of obstacles. Then it becomes damp and slimy, then very dusty, then full of cobwebs and flying bats and scurrying mice. The passage becomes narrower and narrower, and finally grows so narrow that the actors can no longer move. They push outward on the walls, but mysteriously, the walls are growing inward. Finally, the actors discover a rope hanging from the ceiling and they pull down on it. Suddenly, they are freed. The light is so bright their eyes hurt.

They discover they are in a large, beautiful room, the most beautifully furnished room they have ever entered, with high, curtained windows, fireplaces, Persian rugs. The actors discover that they are elegantly dressed. They find food — their favorite kinds — on a buffet. They see friends in the room and greet each other warmly, *in pantomime*. They share, *in pantomime*, their recent adventures. Time passes. The guests party, grow tired and depart.

Imaginative Journey #3

After the actors have stood up, ask them to imagine the following:

They walk away from the beach, down a short road and into a town. It is still a beautiful, sunny day, and they are in great spirits. The actors each see someone they know; they form pairs. They greet each other and tell each other, *in pantomime*, some wonderful thing that has happpened to them that day. Actors should take care to pantomime listening and reacting, as well as talking. The pairs break up and the actors continue individually through town.

The mood changes as they walk farther; the actors glance at their watches: they are late for an important appointment! Everyone else is too slow for them as they rush through the crowded streets. They bump into good friends; they greet each other cordially but hurriedly, and explain, *in pantomime*, their reasons for having to rush off, apologize for their hurry, and leave each other. They continue to rush to their appointment, and discover when they get there that the door is locked — out to an early lunch.

Again, the mood changes. They feel angry, frustrated, and walk through the town, mad at the world. They see acquaintances they don't like, but toward whom they feel they must act politely. They form pairs, grudgingly exchange greetings, explain, *in pantomime*, their foul moods and separate. As they continue on their grouchy paths, they suddenly spot a "sale" sign — 50 percent off something they have wanted for a long time.

Again, the mood changes. They check their wallets — yes, they have enough money! They enter the store and purchase the item. They walk out, happily carrying their new possessions. They meet good friends and tell each other, always pantomiming and never speaking, about their good fortune. They invite each other for a soft drink or an ice cream in a nearby restaurant.

Imaginative Journey #4

After the actors have stood up, ask them to imagine the following, and respond:

They wander away from the beach to the foothills of some beautiful snowcapped mountains. They look far and wide at the mountains that now surround them in every direction. They decide to pack a picnic lunch and go for a hike. They carefully choose fruit and drinks from a cabinet that has just materialized; they make thick sandwiches and cut slices from their favorite cake, and wrap everything up and put it into baskets.

Then they begin to climb up through the mountains. The path winds up and up, and it zigzags back and forth. Occasionally, the actors stop to look out at the beautiful scenery, catch their breath and wipe their brows. On the path, they each meet a friend. They exchange, *in pantomime*, their plans for the day and decide to continue on together. They climb higher and higher, occasionally helping each other over steep sections of the path. They grow tired. It is warm and sunny. They find a picnic spot and sit down, admiring the view. They unwrap their lunches and slowly savor the food, sipping the drinks and eating the sandwiches. It is very still and warm. They look at the scenery.

Suddenly, they both think they hear something, something unusual. They turn to each other, questioning each other with their eyes. They hear nothing and return to their picnic. Suddenly, they hear the sound again, louder: they realize they are hearing the sound of an avalanche. They react — how? Catching hold of one another? Racing away? Trying to hide?

You can easily develop your own imaginative journeys, or the actors can write and lead their own. The main requirements are that the situations be exaggerated enough to imagine and respond to quickly, in pantomime, and that interaction between the actors be kept to a minimum.

Living Patterns and Live Machines

This exercise works well after some work with the relaxation exercise and imaginative journeys outlined previously. Divide the participants into groups of five. Ask each group in turn to stand on the stage in a loose cluster and do the following, in order and without planning:

- Arrange themselves in any pattern, but they must stand upright and face either full front, full back or profile. They freeze in position. They arrange themselves into a new pattern. Freeze. Change patterns again. Freeze.

- Arrange themselves into any pattern, but they can only stand in quarter positions and must remain upright. Freeze. Change patterns. Freeze. Change patterns. Freeze.

- Arrange themselves in any pattern, in any relation to the audience, and bending in various directions from the waist. Freeze. Change patterns. Freeze. Change. Freeze.

- Arrange themselves in any pattern, in any relation to the audience or to each other and with full freedom to put their arms and legs into any position. Freeze. Change. Freeze. Change. Freeze.

- Arrange themselves into any pattern, any position, but each actor must touch at least one other actor. Freeze. Change. Freeze. Change. Freeze.

ange themselves into any pattern and begin to function as
atest machine from science fiction. Add some sound effects!
Everyone make a different sound! Freeze. Change positions.
Begin a new machine.

- Arrange themselves in a pattern and begin to function as an
aggression machine . . . a sadness machine . . . a love machine
. . . a clown machine. Encourage sound effects!

PANTOMIME GAMES

The Selling Game —
or the "Bulgarian Game"

Performance: This is a very easy game, and it appeals strongly to
younger performers — sixth- and seventh-graders. One person goes in
front of the audience. Those in the audience pretend that they are all
Bulgarians — or some other nationality that would not understand
any language that anyone in the group might speak in real life — and
cannot speak English.

The actor pretends that he or she is traveling in Bulgaria and must
buy a particular item, which must be described *through pantomime* to
the "Bulgarians" until they can guess what it is. You can give the
actors items to pantomime, or they can think up their own. If they
choose the latter course, they write their items down on a slip of paper
and turn it in before they go on stage.

In this exercise, unlike in the other guessing pantomimes,
audience members can call out their answers as soon as they decide
upon an answer. The person or persons guessing correctly can then be
the next to perform.

*Advance preparation: Put the suggested items on cards. Be sure
to get them back!

Suggested items:

- car jack
- can of motor oil
- can of bug spray/
  room deodorizer
- ballet toe shoes
- candy bar
- lipstick
- tape recorder
- bookends

- sunglasses
- chain saw
- bird cage
- watering can
- stapler
- curtains
- TV antennae
- spaghetti
- roller skates

- overcoat
- clipboard
- clock
- squirt gun

- flashlight batte
- lamp/sunlamp
- baby bottle

Who Began

This game also enjoys amazing popularity.

Performance: Actors stand in a circle, except one, who is dubbed "detective" and leaves the room. Once this individual is out of sight and hearing, silently indicate one member of the circle to be the "leader." This leader begins a movement, such as tapping a foot, waving hands or swinging arms, and the others in the circle imitate it exactly. The detective then returns and stands in the center of the circle. As soon as the detective is in the center, the leader must change the movement, and the others must immediately follow suit. The detective then guesses "who began." If he/she guesses incorrectly, the leader again changes the movement. The detective gets three chances to guess.

Purpose: This exercise helps the actors to attend carefully to each other and to become absorbed totally in the "stage" action. If the group interacts as a whole, it will almost always fool the detective.

Mirrors
Suggestions for conducting mirror games: In a mirror game, one actor or group takes the role of a person looking into an imaginary mirror; another actor or group plays the role of the reflection.

In these games, encourage silence as much as possible; young performers tend to giggle and cut up unless the atmosphere is controlled. Take some time to demonstrate this activity, using yourself as the person and a volunteer as the reflection. From this demonstration, three guidelines emerge: (1) the person must move *very slowly*; (2) actors should maintain eye contact and rely on peripheral vision, and not try to watch the specific hands or knees; and (3) the left hand of the reflection imitates the right hand of the person. No one can correctly shake hands with his or her mirror image.

Finally, the following position makes a good starting point: actors face each other across the mirror, elbows bent, hands stretched out toward each other, feet slightly apart and weight evenly distributed.

If actors complain they can think of nothing to do, they can try two approaches: they can just move spontaneously, trying to bend, twist, stretch and move their bodies in as many different ways as possible; or they can do any activity that might normally take place in front of a mirror, such as brushing teeth, lifting weights, trying on hats.

Duet Mirror Games

Performance: Actors quickly pair off. The person begins a series of movements and motions — the bigger and more exaggerated, the better — and the reflection imitates them. After about a minute, call out, "Freeze!" The actors freeze into positions. Then call out, "Reverse roles!" Beginning from their frozen positions, the actors trade roles and continue. Keep calling out *freeze* and *reverse* for a few more times, varying the length between each instruction.

Circle Mirror

Performance: All actors stand in a circle. They pretend that they are looking into a large circular mirror. One actor is selected as the person; the rest are reflections. After about 30 seconds, call out, "Freeze!" and name a new person. Beginning from their frozen positions, actors then imitate the motions of the new leader.

Purpose: This exercise, like the "Who Began" game, helps to build group concentration.

REHEARSED PANTOMIME SCENES

Group Mirror Pantomime

Performance: Working in groups of four, actors pantomime a scene in which two characters do something together in front of a "mirror," and the other two reflect their actions.

Example: A barber shaves or cuts the hair of a customer, and a mirror image reflects the action. (In one macabre version, the barber ends the scene by slitting the customer's throat and sinisterly beckoning to the next victim.)

Preparation time: 30 minutes

Performance time: two to five minutes

Stage materials: chairs

Suggestions for conducting the activity: Before the session, have the actors list situations in which activities take place in front of a mirror. The mirror games in the "Short-Short Pantomimes" section (page 38) make a good introduction to this activity.

Visibility may be a problem in these scenes. Encourage the actors to place the "mirror line" straight down the center of the stage. To be easily seen, actors cheat out, experiment with levels (one actor sitting, one standing) and angles (downstage actor positions himself/herself farther away from the mirror than the upstage actor).

Additional scene ideas: In addition to the examples listed on the following activity worksheet, the following situations could logically take place in front of a mirror.

- making faces
- practicing boxing, fencing, band conducting, sharpshooting
- exercise class
- morning — getting ready for school or work
- doctor giving a physical
- restaurant counter
- shoe store
- artist doing self-portraits
- at the fun house (one person and three images)

Names of   *Bette Frank*   *Kate Blanas*
Group Members: *Amy Osterholm*   *Robin Bowman*

Group Mirror Pantomime
(Activity Worksheet — one per group)

DUE: *Today!*

I. BACKGROUND
(Actors interview each other, using questions below and noting answers on this sheet. Actors should leave extra room when they copy this sheet from the chalkboard.)

1. How do you clean the mirrors around your house?

2. Do you believe in the saying that if you break a mirror, you'll have seven years' bad luck?

3. Have you ever been in a mirror fun house?

4. If all the mirrors in the world disappeared tomorrow, what would be the greatest change in our lives?

5. Have you ever looked through a two-way mirror?

II. IDEAS FOR MIRROR PANTOMIMES
(two per person)

1. *barber and customer*
2. *beautician and customer*
3. *two kids cleaning mirrors at home*
4. *customer trying on hats, and salesclerk*
5. *customer trying on coats, and salesclerk*
6. *rock stars putting on make-up*
7. *movie star being made up like a monster*
8. *ballet student and teacher at the barre*

III. CHOSEN IDEAS
Bette & Amy - teacher & student / Kate & Robin - images in Mirror

IV. ACTION SUMMARY
(three to five sentences)
Teacher warms up. Student enters. Teacher demonstrates ballet steps and student repeats them.

Group Focus Pantomime

Performance: Groups of four or five actors pantomime a scene in which they focus their attention on an imaginary offstage object, event or person. Titles are given the scenes to identify what the actors focus on.

Example: Using a sign or an announcement, actors give the title of their scene: "Burning Building." Two begin on stage, watching and reacting. Three others enter and join the group of onlookers; one finds a fire alarm and sounds it. The actors react individually — with horror, with fear, with fascination.

Preparation time: 15 to 25 minutes

Performance time: two minutes

Stage materials: chairs

Suggestions for conducting the activity: Frequently in a script or scene, the action calls for a group of characters to focus their attention on an imaginary offstage object, person or event. This occurs constantly in movies and TV. Two stage examples are the Wells Fargo wagon scene from *Music Man* and the ascot race from *My Fair Lady*.

When several novice actors look at what is supposed to be a single point offstage, they often look in divergent directions, producing a comic effect at best. In this assignment, the actors imagine and commmunicate their interest in an offstage event.

In order for all the actors to look at the same point offstage, a real point must be chosen in advance. For example, the *exit* sign or clock at the rear of the rehearsal hall is an airplane; the edge of the curtain is a tree. If the actors are to react simultaneously in shock or joy, some signal must be prearranged — one actor puts his/her hand to his/her cheek, etc. When an object moves, one actor should show the motion by pointing and moving his/her arm.

*****Advance preparation:** Actors collect examples — from TV and movies — of scenes in which characters look at something or someone out of camera range ("offstage").

SAMPLE

Names of
Group Members: *Sandy Stewart, Michelle Vargas*
Kathy Travanti

Group Focus Pantomime
(Activity Worksheet — one per group)

DUE: *Today!*

I. BACKGROUND
(Actors interview each other, using questions below and noting answers on this sheet. Actors should leave extra room when they copy this sheet from the chalkboard.)

1. What have you seen in your life (not on TV) that you looked at very long and carefully? Were you scared? Excited?

2. Describe a scene on TV in which a character looked "offstage" and "saw" something.

II. IDEAS FOR THINGS TO LOOK AT
(three per person)

1. *spaceship landing*
2. *witch flying overhead*
3. *birds*
4. *tennis game*
5. *javelin throw*
6. *shark swimming by*
7. *plane crash*
8. *charging rhino*
9. *friend getting off airplane*
10. *friend leaving in car*
11. *scary movie*
12. *shooting star*
13. *rainbow*
14. *hitchhikers watching cars go by*
15. *watching for the bus*
16. *tree falling*

III. CHOSEN IDEAS
saying goodbye and watching a friend leave

IV. ACTION SUMMARY
(three to five sentences)
We shake the imaginary friend's hand, pack the car, open the car door, watch the friend start the car and drive away as we wave.

V. IMAGINARY FOCUS
The car will be the wall calendar.

Fantastic Duet Pantomime!

Performance: Working in pairs, actors pantomime an ordinary situation that undergoes a fantastic, or totally unexpected, illogical and imagination-defying twist. The more outrageous and bizarre the twist, the better.

Examples:

- A dentist tries to extract a tooth, but it refuses to budge. Pliers, rope and finally dynamite are used. The dentist walks away, disgusted, and the tooth falls out by itself.

- A doctor checks a patient's reflexes, and the entire leg flies off and must be reattached.

- A mad scientist wires up a monster, which comes alive and kills the scientist. The monster puts the scientist's body on the table and brings it back to life as another monster.

- Gunmen enter a bank and pass a note to the teller. Teller refuses to give over money, gun fails to go off; gunmen exit, embarrassed. Or: the teller gives the robbers far more money than they had dreamed of receiving, opening up an additional safe and offering them the contents of his or her wallet.

Preparation time: 30 to 90 minutes, depending on how polished the pantomimes will be.

Performance time: three to five minutes

Stage materials: chairs, small table

Suggestions for conducting the activity: To help the actors prepare for this scene, discuss the idea of *fantastic* as opposed to *logical*. Use the examples above as a starting point. As a group, actors can list all the fantastic twists a normal situation might develop. For example, what fantastic things might occur during babysitting or washing clothes?

For the performance, encourage exaggerated facial expressions and movements. The title of the scene does *not* give away the fantastic element, but concentrates on the initial, normal situation: "A Trip to the Dentist's Office," instead of "Immovable Tooth."

SAMPLE

Names of Those
in Pair: *Mark Flanagan, Ted Moore*

Fantastic Duet Pantomime!
(Activity Worksheet — one per pair)

DUE: *Tomorrow!*

I. BACKGROUND
(Actors interview each other, using questions below and noting answers on this sheet. Actors should leave extra room when they copy this sheet from the chalk-board.)

1. What would be the most fantastic thing that could happen to you right now, if you had your choice?

2. What are some fantastic events that have occurred in TV shows or movies you have seen?

II. IDEAS FOR NORMAL SITUATIONS WITH TWO CHARACTERS AND A FANTASTIC TWIST
(five per person)

1. *Two gardeners plant a tree; it grows immediately and comes alive.*

2. *Teller and robber: money is counterfeit*

3. *Babysitter and baby: pacifier does not come out of baby's mouth*

4. *Lady and chauffeur: car drives by itself — flies, sails*

5. *Two lumberjacks: cut down a tree that is rubbery and bends*

6. *Pilot and co-pilot: wings fall off airplane*

7. *Teenager: watches TV and a character walks out of the TV*

8. *Ape and man at zoo: man watches the ape and then enters the cage to exchange suits*

9. *Two cooks make pizza, throw pizzas in air and they don't come down*

10. *Two teenagers ride roller-coaster: it falls apart.*

III. CHOSEN IDEA
babysitter and pacifier

IV. IDEAS TO DEVELOP THE SCENE
(events and details that could occur in the scene; five per person)

1. *Say goodbye to parents*   2. *baby starts screaming*

SAMPLE

[Fantastic Duet Pantomime Worksheet, continued]

3. babysitter tries to give baby some food
4. baby refuses to eat
5. baby throws food on floor
6. babysitter gives baby toys; baby throws toys away
7. babysitter sticks pacifier in baby's mouth
8. pacifier is stuck
9. try crowbar, string, pliers
10. baby swallows pacifier

V. ACTION SUMMARY
(three to five sentences)

Babysitter arrives, meets baby, says goodbye to parents. Babysitter begins to do homework and baby starts to cry. Food and toys do not help. Finally the babysitter gives the child a pacifier. Baby stops crying and goes to sleep. Babysitter tries to remove the pacifier, but it doesn't come out. Baby wakes, wide-eyed. Babysitter pries at the pacifier with a knife — no luck. Baby swallows the pacifier and begins to cry again.

VI. IMAGINARY PROPS
pacifier, door, food, spoon, plate, toys, knife

VII. TITLE
"The Quiet Baby"

In-a-Vehicle Group Pantomime

Performance: A group of five to six actors pantomimes being in a single vehicle. The actors may play themselves or character roles: elderly, young, of a certain occupation, etc.

Example: Actors pantomime riding a subway car. Three actors begin on stage; two are seated, and one is standing, holding on to an imaginary overhead strap. One of the seated actors reads an imaginary newspaper. All move in rhythm to the subway movement. The car makes a stop (actors cue each other with a planned signal, such as the reader lowering the newspaper); one actor exits, two more enter, and the car lurches on its way.

Preparation time: 25 to 60 minutes, depending on the degree of coordination the movement is to have.

Performance time: two minutes

Stage materials: chairs

Suggestions for conducting the activity: As a warm-up activity, actors imagine being in and responding to the action of the following vehicles: limousine, train, small plane in a storm, spaceship, stagecoach, race car, ocean liner. How can they communicate the movement of a particular vehicle? In a submarine or tour bus, what are possible characters and events?

Concentrated rehearsal time is necessary to perfect the movement of a roller coaster ride or bumpy jeep trip. For stops and starts, actors must devise a signal system, and rehearse until nothing is obvious to the audience. Encourage the performers to use exaggerated, bigger-than-life movements.

*Advance preparation: Actors list various types of mass and individual transportation.

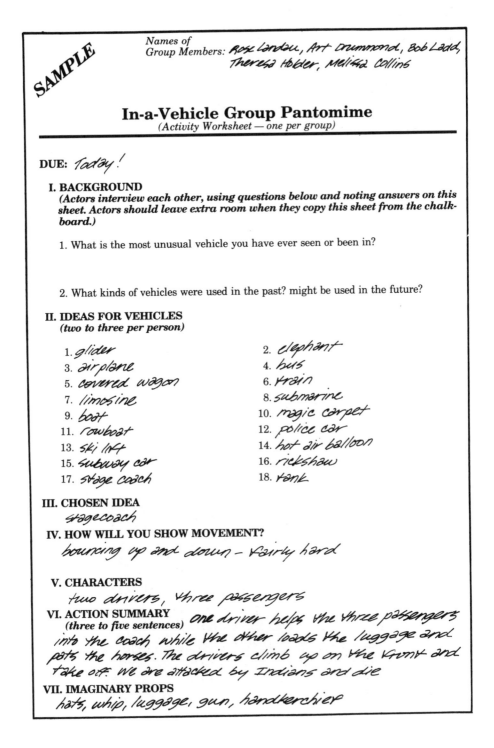

SAMPLE

Names of
Group Members: *Rose Landau, Art Drummond, Bob Ladd, Theresa Holder, Melissa Collins*

In-a-Vehicle Group Pantomime
(Activity Worksheet — one per group)

DUE: *Today!*

I. BACKGROUND
(Actors interview each other, using questions below and noting answers on this sheet. Actors should leave extra room when they copy this sheet from the chalkboard.)

1. What is the most unusual vehicle you have ever seen or been in?

2. What kinds of vehicles were used in the past? might be used in the future?

II. IDEAS FOR VEHICLES
(two to three per person)

1. *glider*
2. *elephant*
3. *airplane*
4. *bus*
5. *covered wagon*
6. *train*
7. *limosine*
8. *submarine*
9. *boat*
10. *magic carpet*
11. *rowboat*
12. *police car*
13. *ski lift*
14. *hot air balloon*
15. *subway car*
16. *rickshaw*
17. *stage coach*
18. *tank*

III. CHOSEN IDEA
stagecoach

IV. HOW WILL YOU SHOW MOVEMENT?
bouncing up and down — fairly hard

V. CHARACTERS
two drivers, three passengers

VI. ACTION SUMMARY
(three to five sentences) *one driver helps the three passengers into the coach while the other loads the luggage and pats the horses. The drivers climb up on the front and take off. We are attacked by Indians and die*

VII. IMAGINARY PROPS
hats, whip, luggage, gun, handkerchief

Be-a-Vehicle Group Pantomime

Performance: Using sound effects, a group of five to six actors pantomimes a *single* large, moving vehicle. One actor may, if necessary, portray a driver or passenger, but the others form the vehicle itself.

Example: Five actors pantomime one large airplane. Two bend at the waist and become the wings, while three line up for the fuselage. The front actor stiffly swings his or her arms for the propeller. The group begins by kneeling; the propeller begins to spin and the plane takes off, making the appropriate noises. The plane banks and turns, encounters rough weather, and makes a bumpy landing.

Preparation time: 30 to 40 minutes

Performance time: two to five minutes

Stage materials: chairs

Suggestions for conducting the activity: Beginning actors often greet this assignment with incredulity ("Do *what?*"), but once they grasp the idea, see a demonstration and experiment on their own, they invent very creative ways of showing a vehicle.

The biggest stumbling block in this assignment is choosing *how* to represent a particular vehicle. First, imagine a vehicle and break it down into recognizable parts: cars have wheels, a steering wheel, hood and stick shift; sailboats have rudders, tillers and sails; helicopters have rotors; steam engines have smokestacks. Then assign actors for specific parts. As a warm-up activity, the entire group can brainstorm ways of representing one or two vehicles.

*****Advance preparation:** Actors observe vehicles, paying particular attention to each vehicle as organized into parts.

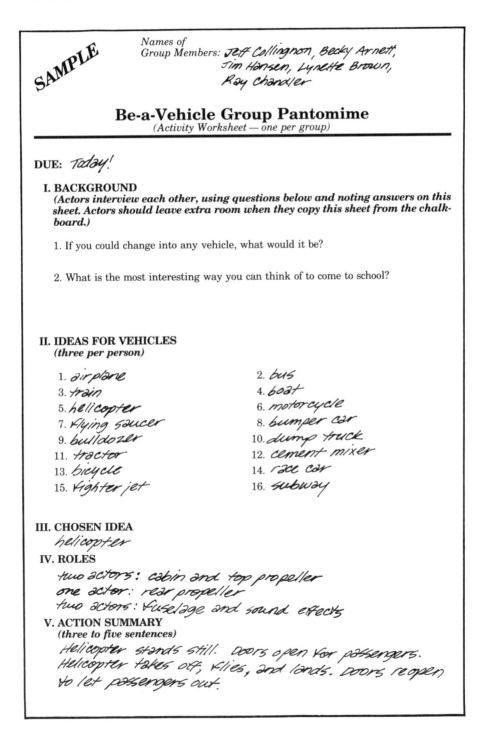

SAMPLE

Names of
Group Members: Jeff Collingnon, Becky Arnett,
Jim Hansen, Lynette Brown,
Ray Chandler

Be-a-Vehicle Group Pantomime
(Activity Worksheet — one per group)

DUE: *Today!*

I. BACKGROUND
(Actors interview each other, using questions below and noting answers on this sheet. Actors should leave extra room when they copy this sheet from the chalkboard.)

1. If you could change into any vehicle, what would it be?

2. What is the most interesting way you can think of to come to school?

II. IDEAS FOR VEHICLES
(three per person)

1. airplane
3. train
5. helicopter
7. flying saucer
9. bulldozer
11. tractor
13. bicycle
15. fighter jet

2. bus
4. boat
6. motorcycle
8. bumper car
10. dump truck
12. cement mixer
14. race car
16. subway

III. CHOSEN IDEA
helicopter

IV. ROLES
two actors: cabin and top propeller
one actor: rear propeller
two actors: fuselage and sound effects

V. ACTION SUMMARY
(three to five sentences)
Helicopter stands still. Doors open for passengers.
Helicopter takes off, flies, and lands. Doors reopen
to let passengers out.

Be-a-Household-Appliance
Group Pantomime

Performance: Making appropriate sound effects, five to seven actors together pantomime a single, large household appliance. One actor may operate the appliance.

Example: Six actors represent a blender. Two of them stand in profile, opposite from each other, with their arms stretched out in a circle around a third actor, who represents the blade. A fourth person stands on a chair behind these three and acts as the lid. The last two actors kneel in front and hold up their fists as pushbuttons. The pantomime begins with an empty blender; the lid opens, something is added with a "glip-glop," as the blades show being hit by something. The blender is activated, first at slow speed, then at high speed, and finally, it stops. The lid opens, and the blender sides bend over to show the liquid being poured out.

Preparation time: 20 minutes

Performance time: two minutes

Stage materials: chairs

Suggestions for conducting the activity: As with the "Be-a-Vehicle" pantomimes, demonstration, brainstorming and encouragement bring creative results. In addition, encourage sound effects. For a warm-up, have the group produce sound effects for various machines: percolators, calculators, vacuum cleaners, vending machines, typewriters, lawnmowers. How is increasing speed represented? a mechanical breakdown?

Once again, the key to this exercise is breaking down a machine into different moving parts, each portrayed by an individual actor. In addition, even a pantomime with a single machine as the main character can present interesting action. Actors should strive to show all possible functions (fill, wash, drain, rinse and spin, for a washer), speeds (fast, slow and medium) and states (on and off) of their chosen machine.

*Advance preparation: Actors observe and collect examples of household appliances they see or use at home.

SAMPLE

Names of
Group Members: *Fred Simms, Louise Wood,*
John Bromley, Lisa Quigley

Be-a-Household-Appliance Group Pantomime
(Activity Worksheet — one per group)

DUE: *Today!*

I. BACKGROUND
(Actors interview each other, using questions below and noting answers on this sheet. Actors should leave extra room when they copy this sheet from the chalkboard.)

1. What appliances do you use at home?

2. If you were an appliance, what would you be?

II. IDEAS FOR APPLIANCES
(two to three per person)

1. *toaster*
2. *sewing machine*
3. *dryer*
4. *vacuum cleaner*
5. *washing machine*
6. *stereo system*
7. *can opener*
8. *electric toothbrush*
9. *alarm clock*
10. *dishwasher*
11. *lawnmower*
12. *mixer*
13. *television*
14. *blender*
15. *typewriter*
16. *hair dryer*
17. *popcorn popper*
18. *coffee maker*
19. *telephone*
20. *shaver*

III. CHOSEN IDEA
sewing machine

IV. ROLES
one actor: needle   two actors: front end of machine
two actors: back end and fly wheel

V. ACTION SUMMARY
(three to five sentences)

Machine begins working. It stiches in a straight line, then zigzags; it speeds up and then stops because the needle breaks.

Be-an-Animal Group Pantomime

Performance: A group of six to nine actors pantomimes a single animal that moves across the stage. Sound effects are encouraged.

Example: Seven performers act out an elephant. Three form the head, with one actor for each ear and one for the trunk. The other four represent the legs and tail. The elephant lumbers heavily around the stage, picking up peanuts with its trunk and trumpeting loudly.

Preparation time: 20 to 25 minutes

Performance time: two to three minutes

Stage materials: chairs

Suggestions for conducting the activity: As with the "Be-a-Vehicle" and "Be-a-Household-Appliance" exercises, group brainstorming and some coaching help overcome the occasional reactions of "We can't do this!" Larger groups work best for this activity. Each group should try to get its animal to do as much as possible — sit down, eat, settle down to sleep, make noises. Inevitably, some group will want to represent *all* bodily functions; a few words about tastefulness on stage might be necessary.

An excellent way to end this session is with the entire class of performers forming one huge mythical beast — a winged dragon, for example.

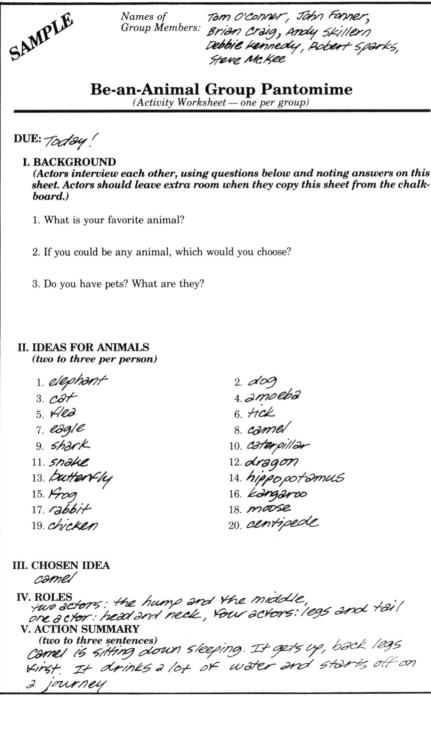

SAMPLE

Names of Group Members: *Tom O'Conner, John Fonner, Brian Craig, Andy Skillern Debbie Kennedy, Robert Sparks, Steve McKee*

Be-an-Animal Group Pantomime
(Activity Worksheet — one per group)

DUE: *Today!*

I. BACKGROUND
(Actors interview each other, using questions below and noting answers on this sheet. Actors should leave extra room when they copy this sheet from the chalkboard.)

1. What is your favorite animal?

2. If you could be any animal, which would you choose?

3. Do you have pets? What are they?

II. IDEAS FOR ANIMALS
(two to three per person)

1. *elephant*
2. *dog*
3. *cat*
4. *amoeba*
5. *flea*
6. *tick*
7. *eagle*
8. *camel*
9. *shark*
10. *caterpillar*
11. *snake*
12. *dragon*
13. *butterfly*
14. *hippopotamus*
15. *frog*
16. *kangaroo*
17. *rabbit*
18. *moose*
19. *chicken*
20. *centipede*

III. CHOSEN IDEA
camel

IV. ROLES
two actors: the hump and the middle, one actor: head and neck, four actors: legs and tail

V. ACTION SUMMARY
(two to three sentences)
Camel is sitting down sleeping. It gets up, back legs first. It drinks a lot of water and starts off on a journey

Solo Pantomime

Performance: A single actor pantomimes an activity that has a beginning, complications and an ending. Before the scene, he or she announces the title of the scene or holds up a sign.

Example: An actor pantomimes playing pinball. He/she walks in, selects a machine, finds his/her money, inserts a coin and begins to play. He/she moves with precision and exaggerated motions. He/she may take on a character — very shy and nervous, or very confident and cool. He/she positions the imaginary machine so it is between himself/herself and the audience. As the actor plays the game, his/her facial expressions and actions reveal whether he/she is winning. He/she wins the first game, loses the second, kicks the machine and walks away.

Preparation time (at home): three to four days

Performance time: two to three minutes

Stage materials: Chairs, small tables. All hand props and costumes, including pockets, should be mimed.

Suggestions for conducting the activity: This activity is one of the few homework activities in this book. The group should try some of the "Short-Short" pantomime activities and the group pantomimes before attempting solo work.

Choosing an interesting activity is the first step; developing a story and interesting action is the second; and rehearsal is the third.

Once chosen, an idea should be exploited for all its possibilities. Exactly what does a person *do* when he/she washes windows or drives a car? What complications or problems might arise when someone waters the garden or buys a candy bar from a machine? What solutions are tried but fail to work? How are the problems finally solved?

Actors should rehearse their pantomimes at least five or six times at home — alone, in front of a mirror or for a friend. They pay attention to details, such as consistent size and shape of objects, visibility and strong, clear facial expressions and gestures. Adequate rehearsal ensures a confident, energetic performance in which the actor, and hence the audience, is completely absorbed in stage action. During a session, actors can pair off and perform in turn for each other. Members of each pair coach each other on precise movements. They help each other answer the question: Am I communicating what I think I am?

*Advance preparation: As group members go about their daily lives, they can make mental lists of activities they perform during the day.

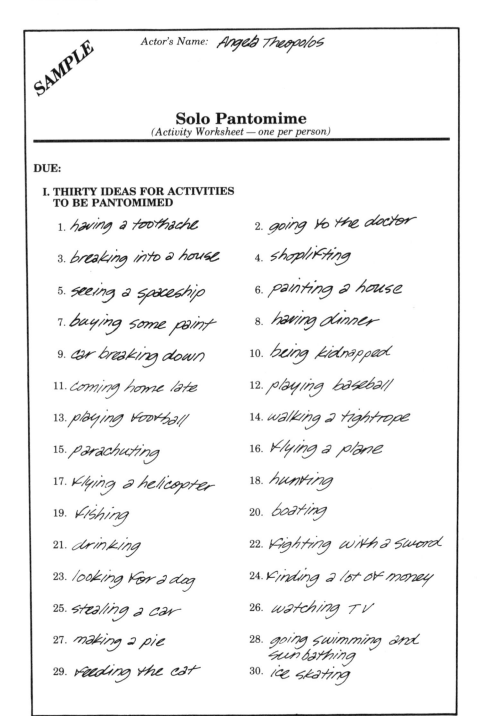

SAMPLE

Actor's Name: *Angela Theopolos*

Solo Pantomime
(Activity Worksheet — one per person)

DUE:

**I. THIRTY IDEAS FOR ACTIVITIES
TO BE PANTOMIMED**

1. having a toothache
2. going to the doctor
3. breaking into a house
4. shoplifting
5. seeing a spaceship
6. painting a house
7. buying some paint
8. having dinner
9. car breaking down
10. being kidnapped
11. coming home late
12. playing baseball
13. playing football
14. walking a tightrope
15. parachuting
16. flying a plane
17. flying a helicopter
18. hunting
19. fishing
20. boating
21. drinking
22. fighting with a sword
23. looking for a dog
24. finding a lot of money
25. stealing a car
26. watching TV
27. making a pie
28. going swimming and sunbathing
29. feeding the cat
30. ice skating

SAMPLE

[Solo Pantomime Worksheet, continued]

II. CHOSEN IDEA
watching TV

III. TEN IDEAS FOR DETAILS
AND COMPLICATIONS

1. after school

2. get something to drink

3. supposed to do homework

4. look in TV GUIDE

5. switch on TV

6. change channels

7. watch excitedly

8. spill softdrink on book

9. problems with reception

10. decide to do homework

IV. ACTION SUMMARY
(three to five sentences) I come home and start my homework. It's boring, so I turn on the TV and watch a good show. I hear my Mom coming home. I turn off the set and begin to do my homework.

V. PROPS

A. Imaginary Props TV, books, pencil, TV GUIDE

B. Set Props two chairs, small table

VI. TITLE "Hard at Work"

VII. FLOORPLAN
(solid line for real set props; dotted line for imaginary set props)

Solo Pantomime to Music

Performance: The actor pantomimes a scene with a beginning, complications and an ending, using an appropriate musical background.

Example: The actor pantomimes a baker, who tries several times to bake a cake, but without success. Music: "Tragedy," by the Bee Gees. The action is timed so that the refrain of "tragedy!" punctuates each new disaster from the oven.

Preparation time: two weeks, with the idea sheet turned in one week in advance.

Performance time: two to seven minutes

Stage materials: chairs, small table

Suggestions for conducting the activity: Warm-up work during sessions prior to this assignment helps the actors prepare for this scene. About three weeks before the performance date, ask the actors to start thinking about music they like and to imagine actions for which such music would provide a background. Ask them to watch scenes on TV and in movies that have no dialogue — only accompanying music. How does the music add to the atmosphere and meaning of the action? What mood does it convey?

During a session, play a few minutes of music and ask the actors to list and share events that could go with the music. Highly varied, dramatic music, such as that from "Zorba the Greek," "West Side Story," Holst's "The Planets," Bartok's "Concerto for Orchestra" and the Moody Blues' "Threshold of a Dream" are possible choices.

Actors fare better if they choose their music first, and then decide on the action. In assigning the project, encourage the actors to open themselves to all types of music — classical, jazz, rock, folk, country, easy listening and movie theme. As tactfully as possible, point out that some music, like hard rock, is better for listening enjoyment than for scene music. Music with repetitious beat and melody is best avoided. Like the scene itself, the music should start, build to a climax and come to an end. Classical pieces or instrumental pieces from musicals and movies lend themselves to pantomime work.

Obviously, action done in time to the music is satisfying to watch. Slamming a door at the same time the timpani crashes, sweeping the floor in rhythm to a waltz, or stirring batter to the tune of the gym dance from *West Side Story* gratifies an aesthetic sense. However, *strongly discourage* actors from presenting, word for word, the action described by song lyrics. The results are uniformly awkward. For example, actors should *not* attempt to reenact the events described in "Ode to Billy Joe," "Harper Valley PTA" or "Coward of the County." On the other hand, songs with lyrics need not be completely ruled out. "Surf

City, U.S.A.," by the Beach Boys, provides a good accompaniment to a surfing pantomime; and "Hitching a Ride" works fine for a hitchhiking scene.

The pantomimes should have a beginning, middle and ending. Actors should bring their own music and prepare a title sign.

*Advance preparation: Collect three or four sound recordings to use in warm-up activities.

SAMPLE

Actor's Name: *Randy Nathan*

Solo Pantomime to Music
(Activity Worksheet — one per actor)

DUE: *in two weeks*

I. FIVE IDEAS FOR MUSIC
(List or describe specific pieces, not general categories like "country" or "jazz.")

1. *"Cloudburst" – mountain climbing*
2. *"Welcome Back, Kotter" – school teacher*
3. *Beethoven's Fifth Symphony – changing a diaper*
4. *"Junk Food Junkie" – raiding the refrigerator*
5. *"1980" – lifting weights*

II. CHOSEN SONG
"1980" – lifting weights

III. TEN IDEAS FOR DEVELOPING THE SCENE

1. *drop weight on toes*
2. *use small hand weights*
3. *hold heavy weight with one hand*
4. *warm-up exercises*
5. *hop around and lift weight*
6. *use "stretch" weights*
7. *win a prize*
8. *show I'm number one*
9. *choose a weight*
10. *fall over backwards*

IV. SCENE INFORMATION

A. Character
myself

B. Setting
weight room

C. Imaginary Hand Props
weights, jump rope

SAMPLE

[Solo Pantomime to Music Worksheet, continued]

   D. Set Props
      none
   E. Title
      "Champ"

V. FLOORPLAN

CHAPTER IV
VOICE

INTRODUCTION

Probably the single greatest weakness in beginning adolescent actors is poor voice control. Reared on the subtle nuances of TV and movie camera work, young actors have difficulty appreciating and develping an adequate stage vocal range. Actors soon find, however, that on the stage, *how* something is said is as crucial as *what* is said. It is helpful, therefore, to spend several sessions on activities that focus on the voice alone and don't even involve stage movement. Short vocal warm-ups, in particular, should be incorporated into all remaining sessions.

Note that the group leader can forcefully demonstrate the power of how something is said, as opposed to what is actually said, by using the following tactic: Relate some totally mundane event — e.g., buying a head of lettuce in a grocery store — but in a secretive, suspenseful voice. Effectively done, the tale will have the listeners on the edge of their seats — until the final moment when they realize they've been duped. Then reiterate that it's not *what* is said, it's *how* something is said, that communicates.

In telling the story, take care to build, in tones of suspense and urgency, a series of events to a totally anticlimactic ending. For example:

"It was a quiet, sunny day, perfect for what I had in mind. I swiftly drove the car to the large, spacious building at the corner of Main and Second Avenue. I parked and hurried in. I walked down the long, crowded aisles until I found the section I was searching for. I glanced around. There it was! I moved silently toward it, and quickly put my hand around — a head of lettuce."

CHARACTERISTICS
OF A GOOD STAGE VOICE

1. **rate:** Almost 90 percent of beginning speakers are nervous and speak too fast. It is useless to tell performers, after their presentation, that they spoke too quickly. They must be interrupted and coached, however briefly, during their performances. Usually, just calling out "too fast" suffices. Other effective measures include repeating a sentence at the correct pace for the performer to imitate, or asking the performer not to say or read the next sentence until you give a signal.

2. **projection:** Most beginning perfomers speak too softly on stage, no matter how noisy they are off stage. Nervousness, inexperience and poor breathing all contribute to a lack of projection. To reduce vocal strain, encourage the actors to yawn and breathe deeply before performing. They should imagine that their voice originates in the waistline area (the diaphragm) and gains volume and tone as it goes through the chest and out through the "megaphone" (mouth). They can also imagine that they are shouting (not screaming) their dialogue over the noise of jackhammers. Again, interrupt or call out "projection!" during performances; the actors need to *feel* the difference between good and poor projection.

3. **clarity:** Garbled speech usually stems from two causes: poor sentence phrasing or poor enunciation. Poor sentence phrasing is a reading problem. Performers with this problem should be encouraged to mark pauses, in the passages they read aloud, with slashes (/) and *not* to pause where there is no slash. Better readers can be enlisted to help with this process.

Poor enunciation is usually just the result of lazy daily speech habits. Beginners tend to slur over consonants, especially the *D/T, G/K* and *B/P* pairs. Also, beginners seldom open their mouths wide enough to produce rounded vowel tones. Tell them they must pass this test: When they say the beginning vowel sounds of words like *Iowa, all* and *over*, they should be able to stick two fingers, held vertically, in their mouths. For these problems, the best remedy is interruption and imitation of the correct sounds. Performing an activity in which everyone overenunciates every single word also helps clear up mushmouth.

4. expression: Beginners are usually too subtle in their expression. Whatever expression they do have, instruct them to overemphasize, to exaggerate as much as possible. At first, they will feel embarrassed, but will gradually feel more comfortable with "being big." Again, interruption and providing a model is best. Listen for a sentence or word the performer has let slip by, interrupt, and repeat the sentence with proper expression. Audience members can record sentences they heard and be invited to perform them with expression.

5. pitch: Adolescent vocal ranges usually undergo so many changes that it's difficult to work too much with pitch at this time. However, all performers should try to use their full range in speaking.

The characteristics listed above apply to *all* performances, improvised or with scripts. In performances that are speeches rather than scenes (such as introductions or the "Advice Column" scenes in this section), performers must meed additional criteria.

6. stance: The performers should stand up straight with weight on both feet, not with their legs crossed or hips tilted. If a manuscript is held, it should be held slightly above waist level. During the performance, manuscripts should be held steadily, not folded, rolled, rustled or dipped up and down.

Wrong   *Right*

Performers should avoid shuffling their feet, rocking back and forth heel-to-toe or turning their feet inward so that body weight is on the outside edges of the feet.

Finally, performers should not begin their presentation until they have come to a full stop in front of the audience, made a slight pause and established eye contact with audience members. This reassures the performers that the audience is ready to hear their presentation. Performers should remain firmly rooted on the stage until they make pause after the very last word of the very last sentence. ⏤eginnings and endings done on the run weaken the overall presentation.

7. **eye contact:** During a prepared presentation, the performer should look out at the audience at least half the time. This requires that the performers practice their selections at least 10 to 15 times before performance.

8. **poise:** In any performing situation, the actors must approach their presentations with confidence in both their ability and preparation. Should a goof occur — and they always do — actors need not register their chagrin to the audience. In particular, immediately after a performance, no matter how badly they feel it has gone, actors must avoid grimacing, giggling, thrusting the manuscript in front of their faces or rolling their eyes upward.

SHORT-SHORT VOICE ACTIVITIES

Vocal Warm-ups

The session leader guides the actors in the following routine. The entire sequence lasts two to three minutes.

A. Actors breathe in slowly; breathe out slowly. They may place their hands around their ribcages and feel how air fills their lungs and pushes out the ribcage. Repeat. Breathe in, and count to 10 aloud.

Variations and additions: Count aloud to 20 or 32 or 46 by twos; to 100 by fives; to 14½ by halves; or backwards, from 17 to zero. Start softly and become loud; start loudly and become soft. Count like a drill sergeant, like a romantic, like a child; count happily, sadly, angrily, boredly, sulkily. Sing like an opera singer; sing like a rock singer on a record played at the wrong speed.

Note: Occasionally, have the actors try to breath in and talk at the same time — it's impossible!

B. Actors pretend their mouths are like rubber bands that stretch in the following sequence: right, left, up, down, drawn in like an old person's mouth, pursed out like a fish's and then stretching in all directions.

Variations and additions: Actors make their faces very small, pushing every feature to a single point, and then make their faces very big, pushing all features out like an inflated balloon. Actors smile a big, dumb smile; frown a big, angry frown; put on a sneer. Actors chew a huge wad of bubble gum.

C. Actors repeat the sequence, "ah, oh, ooh, eeh" (the four basic vowel sounds) two to three times. When they say *ah*, their jaws should be very loose and relaxed, their mouths hanging open, but without strain; at least two fingers' worth of distance should be between the upper and lower teeth. Actors can then add consonants or consonant blends to the beginning or end of these basic vowel sounds, and run through the sequence twice.

For example, placing an *F* at the beginning of each sound produces: "fah, foh, fooh, feeh; fah, foh, fooh, feeh;" placing an *LP* at the end of each sound produces: "alp, olp, oolp, eelp; alp, olp, oolp, eelp." A good series is either the voiced/unvoiced consonant pairs of *F/V*, *B/P*, *G/C*, *D/T*, or all the other "hard" consonants. Working with consonant blends commonly found at the ends of words is also helpful and humorous: *RT*, *RP*, *NT*, *MT*, *TH*, *LM*, *SH*, *CH*, etc. Somehow, the sequence of: "ahrt, ohrt, oohrt, eehrt" is irresistibly funny.

Variations and additions: Ask the actors to "Give me a *T*," or some other consonant or consonant blend, and the actors chant back, "Tah, tah, tah, tah, taaah; tah, tah, tah, tah, taaah." They should make sure their jaws drop and that they are open-mouthed at the end of each series.

D. Actors repeat a short, difficult tongue twister six times.

Sample tongue twisters:

- selfish shellfish
- rubber baby buggy bumpers
- red leather, yellow leather
- knapsack straps
- specific Pacific
- unique New York
- Burgess's Fish Shop Sauce
- Men munch much mush.
- black bug's blood
- Rush the washing, Russell!
- good blood, bad blood
- toy boat
- fruit float
- fresh fried fish
- pre-shrunk shirts

Variations and additions: Repeat six times difficult vocabulary or proper nouns from any current production or lesson. **Examples:** *proscenium, Sophocles, chivalrous, magistrate.*

E. Actors repeat, two to three times, a longer tongue twister written on the board or a sheet of paper, or presented orally by the session leader. Be sure to explain any unknown vocabulary. An excellent source book is *Twist These on Your Tongue* (copyright © 1979 by Joseph Rosenbloom, published by E.P. Dutton, Inc.). These tongue twisters are reprinted by permission:

- Slippery southern snakes slide swiftly down ski slopes.

- Wee Willy whistles to wise Wilber Whale.

- A real red rooster roosts in the rain.

- Beautiful brooks babble between blossoming banks.

- ten terrified tomcats tottering in the tops of three tall trees

- The sixth sheik's sixth sheep is sick.

Color Your Words

The session leader reads or says a list of words in a neutral voice. The actors then repeat the words in chorus, "coloring" them, or saying them with as much appropriate expression as possible, reflecting the actual meaning of the words.

Sample word/phrase list:

cold	angry	harsh
warm	happy	soft
freezing	mad	crackle
sweltering	glad	flow
breezy	sad	rustle
still	tense	smooth
windy	nervous	wavy
stormy	depressed	brisk
calm	at the end of my rope	crunchy
thunder	giggly	silky
dead	weeping	hard
frosty	laughing	gentle
hot	crying	crispy
shivering	grim	brittle
parched	relaxed	spongy
soggy	stern	tender

If the group is working on a production, you can also make a list of "easily colored" words from the script and run through this list with the group.

Color Your Nursery Rhyme

The group leader writes a short nursery rhyme (e.g., "Little Jack Horner," "Little Miss Muffet") on the board. The leader then reads the rhyme in a variety of ways, and the group repeats and imitates each time, in chorus.

Sample ways of reading include:

- suspensefully
- angrily
- sadly
- incredulously
- suspiciously
- nervously
- in a depressed manner
- happily
- like a TV newscaster
- like an advertisement
- as a rock song
- in an operatic voice
- very softly
- very loudly

Greeting by Number

Actors arrange themselves in two lines of equal number, with those in one line facing — from across the room — those in the other line. One side of the room is called *side A*; the other, *side B*. At a signal from the group leader, pairs opposite each other advance toward each other and meet in the middle, greet each other, and cross to the other side.

However, instead of using words of greeting, the actors use numbers. The persons who have come from *side A* always say, "1, 2, 3, 4;" and those from *side B* always say, "5, 6, 7, 8." The persons from *side A* say their numbers as if they were saying, "Hi, how are you?" The persons from *side B* say their numbers as if they were saying, "Fine, thank you very much."

At this point, all group members will profess great confusion; it's time for a demonstration, with you taking the part of *side A* and a volunteer that of *side B*. Begin from opposite sides. Greet each other, using numbers only, and cross to the other side. Have everyone practice twice to nail down the procedure.

Now the fun begins — the actors move across the room, and greet each other in different ways:

- like old enemies
- like snobs

- like long-lost friends
- like people in a big hurry, but friendly
- like rude people in a big hurry
- like business executives
- like old people
- like young children
- sadly, crying
- angrily
- in a bored manner
- extremely politely
- very shyly, scared
- as if on a very cold day/sweltering day
- like drunkards
- while giggling
- with pronounced accents
- like suspicious spies
- like robots

Directed Poetry Reading

Most beginning actors are incredibly unaware of the wide vocal range necessary to make stage speech interesting. Most adolescents feel self-conscious and silly when they add variety to their usual monotones. Therefore, plan to do some fairly expressive reading yourself, with the group imitating you in relatively small segments.

If you have begun with the vocal warm-ups, the group should feel comfortable repeating words and sentences out loud, and will be ready for a longer project.

In working with poems, it is usually best to have copies available for every actor, or to write the poems on the chalkboard. Longer works can be projected with an overhead projector.

However, when you first conduct the activity, begin by reading the poem out loud to the group, as expressively as possible. For this first reading, the actors should *not* have copies of the poem, but should merely listen. Practice the poem a couple of times so you'll be able to make eye contact with your audience and build the poem to an appropriate climax.

After you read the poem, make copies available, and then explain how you've read the poem, stanza by stanza. Explain any unfamiliar vocabulary words; point out words you've emphasized; show how you've built suspense and how you've colored the words to give expression. After you explain a stanza, reread it, and then have the group read it in chorus.

With some of the longer poems, and as the group becomes adept at oral reading, you will not need to explain every stanza or even provide a model for reading it (which, of course, is the ultimate goal).

A good written exercise is for the students to read a poem silently and make a list of words that are easily colored. They can also note where the poem changes its line of thought and what kind of tone each stanza should have.

After you've read through a group of poems, you may want to assign different groups to read aloud or enact individual poems. It is usually better to split the poem into parts and have individual performers read different lines than to have the group read the poem as a chorus.

The most successful poems are story-type poems with plenty of built-in suspense and action. Lyric or romantic or free verse poems seldom fare well with this age group.

Suggested poems:

- "Casey at the Bat." An excellent beginning. Many students, surprisingly, have not read it, and an effective reading will have them on the edge of their chairs.

- "The Spider and the Fly." The allusion is famous, and the contrast in the voice pitches of the spider and the fly is fun to exaggerate.

- "Jim — the Story of a Boy Who Ran Away and Was Eaten by a Lion." This and other poems by Hillaire Belloc are not great literature, but *are* suspenseful and fun to read.

- "Charge of the Light Brigade," by Alfred Lord Tennyson. This poem is especially interesting when the actors try to capture, vocally, the roar of the cannon.

- "The Raven," by Edgar Allan Poe. The group can work out variations of "Nevermore."

- "The Cremation of Sam McGee," by Robert Service.

- "Danny Deever," by Rudyard Kipling.

- All the poems in *Where the Sidewalk Ends*, by Shel Silverstein. These poems are also good to perform for child audiences.

*Advance preparation: Collect copies of the poem. Practice the poetry yourself.

REHEARSED VOICE SCENES

Advice Column Scene #1

Performance: Actors work in pairs. One begins by reading aloud a letter asking for advice, like those written to "Dear Abby" or "Dear Ann Landers." The second performer reads an answer to this problem and then reads a letter about a problem of his or her own. The first performer then reads an answer to the second problem.

Example: First actor reads a letter, describing the problem of shyness, to an advice columnist called "The Wise One." Second actor reads an answer to this problem, taking the role of The Wise One. This second performer then reads a letter addressed to "Advisor Adolf," concerning the matter of smelly shoes. The first actor then reads and answer from "Advisor Adolf."

Performance time: two to four minutes

Preparation time: 30 to 60 minutes

Stage materials: tall stools, if available

Suggestions for conducting the activity: Younger performers, in particular, have difficulty understanding the "who does what when" aspect of this performance, so it's helpful to demonstrate, preferably with a partner, a performance of this activity.

To avoid needless and distracting paper shuffling during the performances, insist that all actors write their own letters, then show the letters to their partners, who should write an answer on another sheet of paper. It is usually not successful for actors to write their own answers and have someone else read them — they tend to have trouble deciphering each others' handwriting and punctuation.

*Advance preparation: Actors look for examples of advice columns in daily newspapers or magazines.

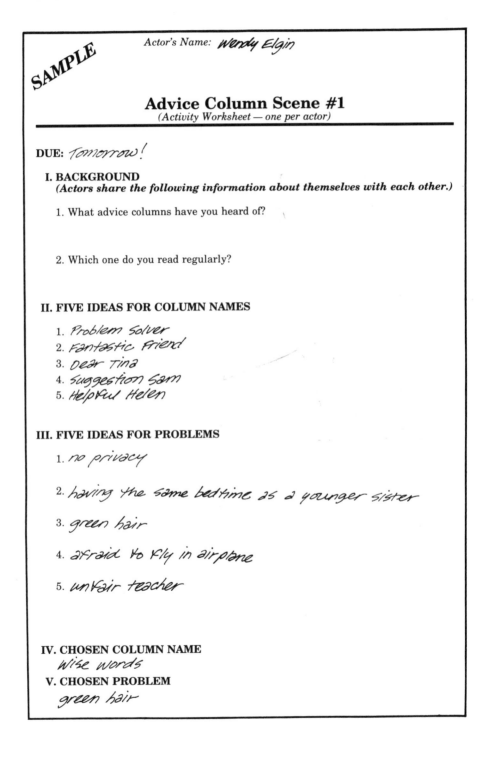

SAMPLE

Actor's Name: *Wendy Elgin*

Advice Column Scene #1
(Activity Worksheet — one per actor)

DUE: *Tomorrow!*

I. BACKGROUND
(Actors share the following information about themselves with each other.)

1. What advice columns have you heard of?

2. Which one do you read regularly?

II. FIVE IDEAS FOR COLUMN NAMES

1. *Problem Solver*
2. *Fantastic Friend*
3. *Dear Tina*
4. *Suggestion Sam*
5. *Helpful Helen*

III. FIVE IDEAS FOR PROBLEMS

1. *no privacy*

2. *having the same bedtime as a younger sister*

3. *green hair*

4. *afraid to fly in airplane*

5. *unfair teacher*

IV. CHOSEN COLUMN NAME
Wise words

V. CHOSEN PROBLEM
green hair

SAMPLE

[Advice Column Scene #1 Worksheet, continued]

VI. FIVE IDEAS FOR DEVELOPING A LETTER ABOUT THE PROBLEM

1. Explain how my hair turned green

2. Tell what I've done so far

3. Ask for help

4. Ask for medicine to cure the problem

5. Ask if there's anything to dye the hair to normal color

VII. SCRIPT

Dear Advisor Ann (name taken from partner),
Last week I had an accident in science class. What happened was that some chemicals got into my hair and turned it bright green, and now the color won't wash out. I've tried several shampoos, but nothing works. Should I dye it another color, or is there a medicine that will get the green out? What should I do?   Signed, Laughed-At

VIII. ANSWER TO PARTNER'S PROBLEM
(See the following activity sheet for partner's letter.)

Dear Twitch,
Here's the solution. Get a large hammer. The next time your leg starts twitching, smash yourself in the kneecap with the hammer. You'll be so occupied with the pain, you won't even care about the twitching!

Signed,
Wise Words

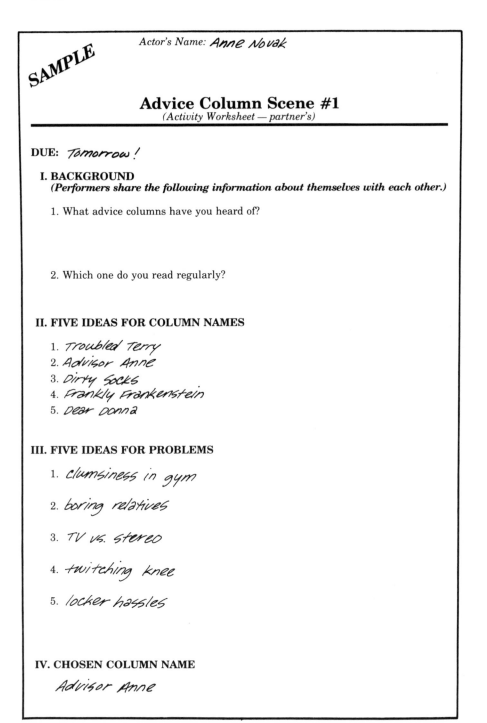

Actor's Name: *Anne Novak*

SAMPLE

Advice Column Scene #1
(Activity Worksheet — partner's)

DUE: *Tomorrow!*

I. BACKGROUND
(Performers share the following information about themselves with each other.)

1. What advice columns have you heard of?

2. Which one do you read regularly?

II. FIVE IDEAS FOR COLUMN NAMES

1. *Troubled Terry*
2. *Advisor Anne*
3. *Dirty Socks*
4. *Frankly Frankenstein*
5. *Dear Donna*

III. FIVE IDEAS FOR PROBLEMS

1. *clumsiness in gym*

2. *boring relatives*

3. *TV vs. stereo*

4. *twitching knee*

5. *locker hassles*

IV. CHOSEN COLUMN NAME

Advisor Anne

SAMPLE

[Advice Column Scene #1 Worksheet, continued]

V. CHOSEN PROBLEM

twitching knee

VI. FIVE IDEAS FOR DEVELOPING A LETTER ABOUT THE PROBLEM

1. *knee twitches uncontrollably*

2. *happened during a skiing accident*

3. *twitches at the wrong times*

4. *afraid I'll hurt someone*

5. *doctors don't help*

VII. SCRIPT *Dear Wise Words (partner's advice column),*

I have a problem that seems impossible to solve. Ever since I hurt my leg skiing, the knee tends to twitch uncontrollably. It often seems to do so at the wrong time — like when a teacher calls on me and I don't know the answer, or during church services. Sometimes it twitches so hard that I'm afraid I'll hurt someone! My doctor says there's nothing I can do, but there must be something! Can you help? Signed, *Twitch*

VIII. ANSWER TO PARTNER'S PROBLEM

Dear Laughed At,

I think you should try to start a fashion of green hair. However, if it doesn't catch on, try dying your hair red. Red and green mixed together make a dark color like brown. If nothing works, you'll have to wear a hat until your hair grows out.

Signed, Advisor Anne

Advice Column Scene #2

Performance: The performance is the same as that for "Advice Column Scene #1," except that the letters should include some dialogue. For example, a letter about conflicts with a younger brother may include an excerpt from a typical argument; a letter about bad customer service may include an excerpt from an exchange between a disgruntled customer and a rude sales clerk.

Example: see worksheet

Performance time: three to five minutes

Preparation time: 40 to 70 minutes

Stage materials: tall stools, if available

Suggestions for conducting the activity: If the actors are unpracticed in punctuating dialogue, provide a written example, using any sample worksheet. Encourage experimentation with variations in pitch, pace, accent and expression between the speakers in the dialogue. Remind the performers that a slight pause comes between the phrase, "He said," and what he actually says.

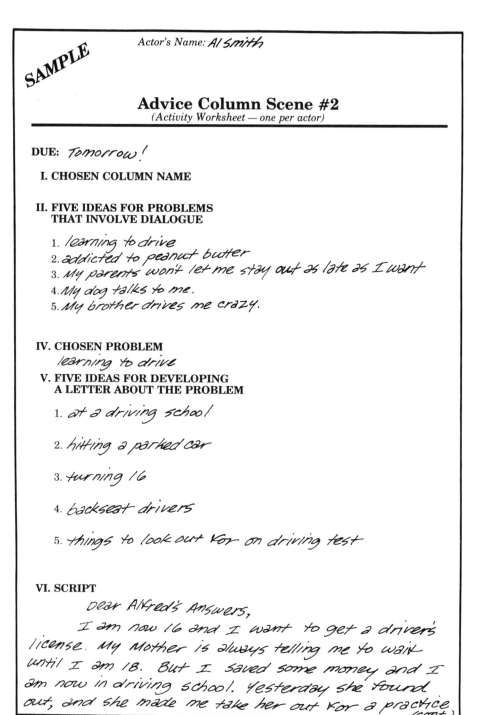

SAMPLE

Actor's Name: *Al Smith*

Advice Column Scene #2
(Activity Worksheet — one per actor)

DUE: *Tomorrow!*

I. CHOSEN COLUMN NAME

II. FIVE IDEAS FOR PROBLEMS
THAT INVOLVE DIALOGUE

1. *learning to drive*
2. *addicted to peanut butter*
3. *My parents won't let me stay out as late as I want*
4. *My dog talks to me.*
5. *My brother drives me crazy.*

IV. CHOSEN PROBLEM
learning to drive

V. FIVE IDEAS FOR DEVELOPING
A LETTER ABOUT THE PROBLEM

1. *at a driving school*

2. *hitting a parked car*

3. *turning 16*

4. *backseat drivers*

5. *things to look out for on driving test*

VI. SCRIPT

Dear Alfred's Answers,

I am now 16 and I want to get a driver's license. My Mother is always telling me to wait until I am 18. But I saved some money and I am now in driving school. Yesterday she found out, and she made me take her out for a practice

(cont.)

SAMPLE

[Advice Column Scene #2 Worksheet, continued]

drive. During the whole time, she kept saying things like, "Slow down, don't hit that curb!" and "Watch out for that red light!" I tried to make her be quiet, but as you can see, I had no luck: "There's a stop sign there." — "Mom, I can see th—" — "Don't forget to stop." — "I've already stopped," I said.

But she goes right on: "And watch out for that car making the turn. And look out behind you in the mirror!"

I am just about to go crazy. What should I do?

Signed,
Always Listening

VII. ANSWER TO PARTNER'S PROBLEM

Dear Needs Help,

I'll be very brief and frank. You're crazy! One hundred percent weirdo! You're nuts! Give up your worm farm! Give yourself over to the authorities! This advice was given with the help of my pet turtle, who is an expert in these matters.

Signed,
Know-It-All and Turtle

SAMPLE

Actor's Name: *James Tilbertson*

Advice Column Scene #2
(Activity Worksheet — partner's)

DUE: *Tomorrow!*

I. CHOSEN COLUMN NAME
Alfred's Answers

**II. FIVE IDEAS FOR PROBLEMS
THAT INVOLVE DIALOGUE**

1. *little brother smarter than older brother*

2. *talking pets*

3. *talking food*

4. *haunted Aunt*

5. *father mad about grades*

III. CHOSEN PROBLEM
talking worms

**IV. FIVE IDEAS FOR DEVELOPING
A LETTER ABOUT THE PROBLEM**

1. *having a worm farm*

2. *worms talk to me*

3. *complaints about their living conditions*

4. *I think I'm crazy.*

5. *They never talk when anyone else is there.*

V. SCRIPT *Dear Know-It-All,*
I have a big problem. People think I'm crazy!!
You see, I'm an earthworm farmer and I believe
(cont.)

SAMPLE

[Advice Column Scene #2 Worksheet, continued]

earthworms can talk. In fact, I talk to them all the time. They are very intelligent, even as intelligent as humans, and they are extremely friendly!! Just to show you how intelligent they are, I have here one of our conversations. I am talking to Walter, whom I've known for a long time: "Hi Walter, what're you doing?" — "I'm eating my lunch now." — "How is it?" — "The dirt here is kind of dry, but that mud over there by the fence is grade A!" — "Here, let me try it. Ummm, it is kind of dry. Needs some salt. By the way, Walter, how's the wife and kids?" — "Oh, fine. Joey is kind of sick. Doctor says it's food poisoning. Looks like some pest killer was mixed in the dirt he ate." — "I hope he gets better. I've got to go now. So long!"

The worms only talk to me, never to anyone else. Now, do you think I'm crazy?

Signed,
Needs Help

VI. ANSWER TO PARTNER'S PROBLEM

Dear Always Listening,

You may simply have to save up your money again and buy your own car, and don't ever let your Mother get the keys or ride with you. Otherwise you might have an accident because she's giving you too much advice.

Signed,
Alfred's Answers

Low-Voice Radio Broadcast

Performance: Each actor makes a short radio broadcast (national, state, city, school — news, weather, community announcements, sports), using a low, deep voice. Since low voices are pleasant to hear and because actors need to practice using their entire vocal range, this is a very useful activity. Performers may sit behind a partition with a large radio visible to complete the effect of a radio broadcast.

Example: Actor announces coming school events.

Preparation time: 20 minutes

Performance time: one minute

Stage materials: Partition or screen to block actors from the audience's view; old radio; tape recorder to record voices if desired.

Suggestions for conducting the activity: Explain the importance of developing voice pitch control, especially in the lower register. Low voices are pleasant to hear and usually carry well. They also sound sinister and powerful when a role calls for those qualities. If you want to repeat this activity, you can simply assign a specific category each time; i.e., commercials, community announcements, etc. You may also assign it as a duet performance.

SAMPLE

Actor's Name: *Tony Jones*

Low-Voice Radio Broadcast
(Activity Worksheet — one per actor)

DUE: *Today!*

TYPE OF BROADCAST: *School News*

I. BACKGROUND
(Actors interview each other — or question themselves — using question below and noting answers on this sheet. Actors should leave extra room when they copy this sheet from the chalkboard.)

What kinds of personalities, moods, events, TV characters and stories do you associate with low voices?

II. FIVE IDEAS FOR NEWS ITEMS

1. *homecoming*
2. *fight in the gym*
3. *locker problems*
4. *vandalism*
5. *fire in the science lab*

III. SCRIPT

Good Evening. This is Tony Jones, reporting the six o'clock news. There was a fire at Lanier Jr. High today. It started in Mr. Ferree's seventh-grade science class, and burned a hole in the ceiling. Mr Ferree simply said, "It had to happen soon."

There was also a fight in the courtyard today. Joe Slow gave Mike Ike a fat lip. Then Mike Ike gave Joe Slow a black eye. The assistant principal came out and Mike and Ike gave him a black eye and a fat lip. The assistant principal then ran home, crying, "Mama, they hit me!"

That's all for now. More at 10. This is Tony Jones at LJH News. Have a good evening.

Interview Scene

Performance: Two actors interview each other, both playing characters other than themselves. They present a total of two scenes, so that they each play both interviewer and interviewee. Actors choose either an on-location or studio setting.

Example: A robot interviews the latest computer on a TV show. Both characters use appropriate voices. The interviewer asks such questions as, "What is your name and number?" or, "What size batteries do you need?" At the end of the interview, the computer goes wild and breaks down.

Preparation time: 30 minutes (per interview)

Performance time: three to six minutes

Stage materials: chairs, table, fake microphone

Suggestions for conducting the activity: This is a good exercise for character and voice development, since the actors need have little concern for stage movement. Emphasize that the interviewer can be as interesting as the interviewee.

Also, stress that most interesting interviews take place when the interviewee has just done something newsworthy, which can be almost anything, from writing a cookbook to opening a dog boutique. In addition, the interview should start from a specific point, such as, "We've heard that you have an unusual hobby. Can you tell us what that is?" The interviewer should ask questions about a unique situation, not just general questions like, "How old are you?" or, "What are your hobbies?"

Furthermore, emphasize that the interview should build to an ending, either logical (the interviewer is out of time; it's time for a commercial break) or surprising (rock-climber falls off cliff at the final question). Performers should avoid product sample interviews and concentrate on interviewing an interesting character.

*Advance preparation: The performers watch TV interview shows or listen to radio interviews and collect sample questions and interesting responses.

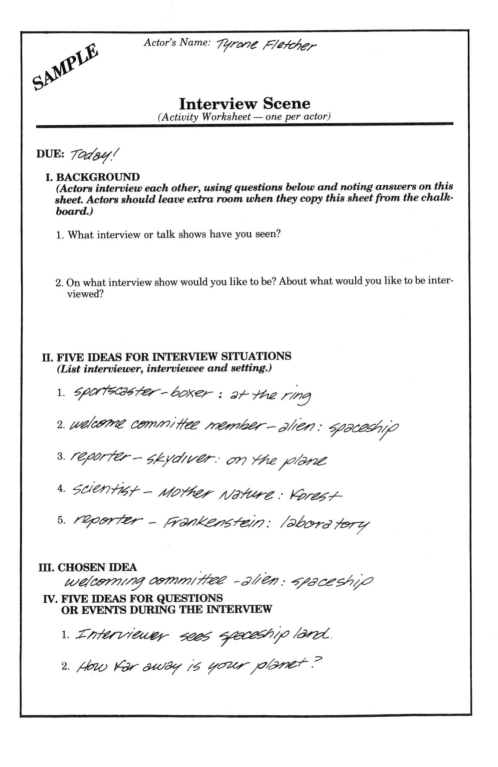

SAMPLE

Actor's Name: *Tyrone Fletcher*

Interview Scene
(Activity Worksheet — one per actor)

DUE: *Today!*

I. BACKGROUND
(Actors interview each other, using questions below and noting answers on this sheet. Actors should leave extra room when they copy this sheet from the chalk-board.)

1. What interview or talk shows have you seen?

2. On what interview show would you like to be? About what would you like to be interviewed?

II. FIVE IDEAS FOR INTERVIEW SITUATIONS
(List interviewer, interviewee and setting.)

1. *sportscaster - boxer : at the ring*

2. *welcome committee member - alien: spaceship*

3. *reporter - skydiver: on the plane*

4. *scientist - Mother Nature: forest*

5. *reporter - Frankenstein: laboratory*

III. CHOSEN IDEA
welcoming committee - alien: spaceship

IV. FIVE IDEAS FOR QUESTIONS
OR EVENTS DURING THE INTERVIEW

1. *Interviewer sees spaceship land.*

2. *How far away is your planet?*

[Interview Scene Worksheet, continued]

SAMPLE

3. Why did you come to earth?

4. Are you interested in a tour of this town?

5. What do you call yourselves?

V. ENDING

Interviewer learns that the alien is on earth
to hunt his favorite food – humans!

VI. SCRIPT/QUESTIONS

Committee Member: Here we are, where a spaceship
has just landed, and I'm talking to a real live alien.
What are you, alien, and where do you come from?

Alien: I come from Pluton and I am called a
Plutonian. My name is Krypton.

Committee Member: About how far is that from earth?

Alien: About a million light centuries away, which
took about two earth days or two Plutonian hours,
to travel.

Committee Member: What is that thing you have in
your hand?

Alien: It's a stun gun. Would you like a demonstration?

Committee Member: Yes, thank you. (Alien points gun at
committee member) Maybe some other time. How old
are you?

Alien: About 2000 earth years.

Committee Member: What did you come to earth for?

Alien: To hunt my favorite food.

Committee Member: And what is that?

Alien: Humans! (Committee member runs off.)

One Word-Three Situations Scene

Performance: Given a single word, such as *please* or *sorry*, a group of three to four performers develops and performs three or four short scenes. Each scene should depict a different situation; in each scene, a different actor says the word or phrase — in a different way. The word is spoken at a high point during the scene, not thrown away in the first few lines.

In an alternative performance, each actor says the given word in a different way within a single scene. For example, each actor says *I guess* within one continuous scene.

Example: Given the word *welcome*, three actors portray the following situations: saying *welcome* to a long-awaited good friend; saying *welcome* to relatives they dislike and whom they greet only at their parents' insistence; saying *welcome* to visiting diplomats.

Preparation time: 10 to 15 minutes

Performance time: three minutes

Stage materials: table, chairs

Suggestions for conducting the activity: First, remind the actors that many words are repeated every day, but how these words are said depends on the situation in which they are spoken. As a group, the actors can repeat words like *sorry* or *never* in as many ways as possible: angrily, sadly, bitterly, happily, boredly, politely, loudly, softly, suspiciously, romantically, regally, roughly, tiredly. They should try for as much exaggeration as possible.

Emphasize that the specific situation is the strongest influence on how something is expressed. Once the actors decide on the situation and characters, they easily discover how their chosen word should be said.

Suggested words/phrases:

- well
- welcome
- never
- so
- I guess
- don't
- good
- thank you
- sorry
- why
- oh, no
- really
- maybe/perhaps
- tell me
- please
- goodbye

*Advance preparation: In their daily lives, actors listen to conversations and note how people say the same words in different ways, according to the particular situation.

SAMPLE

Names of
Group Members: *Mike Latour, Lisa Wong, Larry Hamm*

One Word-Three Situations Scene
(Activity Worksheet — one per group)

DUE: *Today!*

I. REQUIRED WORD/PHRASE   *oh, no*

II. IDEAS FOR SITUATIONS
(two per person)

1. *dropping a bowl of cake batter*

2. *cutting yourself*

3. *realizing you left homework at home*

4. *burning dinner while talking on the phone*

5. *You're halfway to a ski resort when you realize you forgot the skis.*

6. *getting a notice to go to the office*

III. SCENE ONE
(Action Summary: three to five sentences)

1. Setting: *car*

2. Characters: *three skiers*

3. Action Summary: *Three teen-agers are driving toward a ski resort. They stop for hot chocolate and one of them notices that the ski rack has only two pairs of skis on it. They react, "oh, no!"*

IV. SCENE TWO
(Action Summary: three to five sentences)

1. Setting: *kitchen*

SAMPLE

[One Word-Three Situations Scene Worksheet, continued]

    2. Characters: *three cooks*

    3. Action Summary: *Three cooks are preparing a soup — slicing carrots, onions, etc. — when one cuts herself and cries out "oh, no!"*

V. SCENE THREE
(Action Summary: three to five sentences)

    1. Setting: *classroom*

    2. Characters: *teacher, two students*

    3. Action Summary: *Two students are sitting in class when the teacher gives one of them a notice to report to the office. The student reacts, "Oh, no!"*

CHAPTER V
IMPROVISATION & SCENE-BUILDING

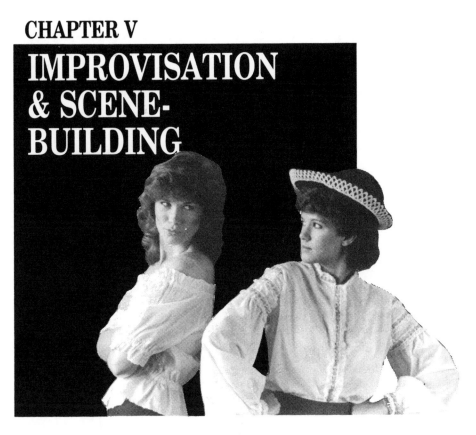

INTRODUCTION

An improvisation is a scene performed with little or no planning. A situation ("You are in a mine shaft and have just heard an explosion.") or structure ("You begin the scene with one emotion, such as anger, and end with another, opposite emotion, such as sadness.") provides the basis of the scene. Junior high-aged actors respond enthusiastically to improvisation if they are given enough of a foundation for an interesting scene. Improvisation can be used as an end in itself; often a group will develop enough material for a show. "Improvs" can also strengthen work with a script.

HINTS FOR IMPROV PERFORMANCES

In developing improvised scenes, actors observe the usual acting criteria for communicating all action and dialogue (see Chapter I, "Terms and Goals for Performers"). In addition, an improvisation must be energetic and suspenseful enough to hold the audience's attention. Inexperienced actors often feel overwhelmed by the dual task of developing and performing a story and dialogue. However, the following hints can aid performance:

1. **Begin the scene with as much energy** as possible, and begin with a definite, exaggerated character in mind. For example, don't play a mere student; choose, instead, to play a very nervous, eager-to-please student; a saccharine teacher's pet; a totally unruffled, somewhat high antiauthoritarian; a giggly harebrain; a sophisticated snob.

2. **Use the body to express character or mood.** Again, exaggerate movement. Try moving slinkily, jerkily, heavily, lightly.

3. **Make vocal choices.** Accents can enliven a scene or lead to ideas for reactions and characterization. Through voice tones, express age and temperament.

4. **In a solo improvisation, keep talking,** as if expressing thoughts aloud. Avoid turning the scene into a pantomime.

5. **In a group improvisation, *listen*** to the other members of the group. Too often, improvs degenerate into shouting matches.

6. **During the scene, do *not ever, ever,*** say, "This is boring," or "What should we do now?" Lines like these clearly reveal a lack of ideas, and they do nothing to inspire action.

HINTS FOR SCENE-BUILDING

Most advice about scene development centers on the requirements of any story: it should have a beginning, middle and an end. All very true, but what does such advice mean? In greater detail, these requirements mean that each scene should contain the following:

1. **an initial situation:** The performers should give details of this situation through dialogue. These details can include the events that have led up to the beginning of the improv. Just mentioning the background events often leads to action within the scene.

   For example, from the basic situation, "police officer stops driver for traffic violation," the actors need to establish the specific traffic violation. They can also define the situation more specifically: rain is pouring down; two whining kids tussle in the back seat; the driver has forgotten his or her license.

2. **complications and suspense:** At some point early in the scene, the actors need to show clearly that the characters want something (the objective) and to fabricate obstacles that stand in the way of reaching that objective. In most western drama, the sequence of objective-obstacle forms the storyline, and audiences expect it from the shortest of improvisations. This does not mean that every improv should be an argument. In the scene based on the traffic violation,

complications can obviously stem from the clash bet~
tive of the police officer (to give a ticket) and that ⟨
avoid getting a ticket).

However, other possibilities exist: the driver could actually be ⌐
bank robber, who readily agrees to all minor charges in hopes of
avoiding the real crime; the officer has stopped the driver to give a
friendly warning, and discovers contraband in the car's back seat;
the whining children help indict the driver; the driver is all-coopera-
tive, but disorganized in finding the correct papers, and rambling
in answering questions.

Another approach to developing complications is to think in terms
of incongruities, or unexpected events. What happens if the patient's
problem is that his son thinks he's a frog, and then a frog hops in?
What happens if the driver turns out to be the police chief?

3. **conclusion:** All improvs must come to an end. The obstacles are
   eventually surmounted and resolved. In solo improvisations, the
   actor can choose a surprise ending: he/she has been pushing against
   a door, only to discover that it opens in the opposite direction. Or
   the actor may choose a logical ending that follows from his/her actions during the scene: after a series of mishaps, the dinner is finally
   ready for the boss; the diary-keeper succeeds in blackmailing the
   younger sibling and extracts a promise never to read the diary again.

In a group improvisation, the actors have the same choices, but they
have the additional burden of communicating their choices to their
partners. Even when rehearsal time is exceptionally brief, actors must
spend a portion of it discussing possible endings. During the performance, actors *must* listen to each other and be prepared to take a hint
that a conclusion has been reached. There comes a time when the police
officer either gives the driver a ticket, lets the driver go or finds a
bigger reason to arrest the driver. At any rate, obstacles or incongruities
must disappear.

SHORT-SHORT IMPROVISATIONS

Add-on Story

Performance: Five performers sit on chairs or on the floor in front of
the group. One begins telling any story that comes into his or her mind.
After 30 seconds to a minute, the session leader selects another performer to continue the story; then a third, and so on, until the last
performer selected completes the story.

Telling a Story and Acting It Out

Performance: A narrator (or pair of narrators) stands to the side of the stage area and tells a story, while a group of five to six performers improvises actions and dialogue from what the narrator(s) says (say).

Variation: One narrator tells a well-known nursery rhyme or fairy tale. The narrator should have a firm grip on the story line — this is no time to hesitate about the ending of "Goldilocks and the Three Bears."

Variation: Two narrators tell a story they make up as they go along. Usually, it is best to have the narrators speak a total of four times, with one narrator beginning the story and the other ending it. This is a good activity to follow the "Add-on Story."

Chain Sentence

Performance: Actors sit in a circle. One begins a sentence by saying a single word. Words like *a, the, and*, and prepositions do not count. Continuing around the circle, each performer adds one word to keep the sentence going until it reaches a logical conclusion.

Variation: In putting together the "Alphabetical Chain Sentence," the same process is followed, but each word must be in alphabetical order.

Join-in Scene

Performance: This activity is similar to "Join-in Pantomimes," except that the performers can speak. One actor goes on stage and begins a scene with a monologue or activity. One by one, other actors join in the action. The total number of players should be limited to five; otherwise, the scene becomes too rambunctious.

Suggestions for conducting the activity: As with the join-in pantomimes, stress cooperative, not combative, activities. Ending these scenes can prove to be a challenge. The last player to join the scene goes on stage with the goal of bringing the scene to a conclusion, and the other four cooperate.

*Advance preparation: Have the list of the pantomime beginnings handy. See page 30.

Continuation Scene

Performance: One actor goes on stage and arranges the available set properties (for example, three chairs) into a setting. He/she sits or stands in a neutral position. A second actor then enters and begins a totally improvised scene. The first actor must react and play along accordingly. After the scene has played for a while, a third actor enters, reacting to and adding to the action on stage. Soon thereafter, the first actor must find some logical way to exit from the scene, leaving the second and third actors on stage. These two actors continue the scene; a fourth actor enters; the second actor eventually exits. This process continues until the last actor to go on stage enters. The scene should then be brought to a conclusion.

Variation: Follow the same procedure, with the exception that the first actor sets the scene into motion instead of remaining neutral.

Variation: Follow the same procedure, with the exception that each additional actor begins an entirely new scene. The actors on the stage must adjust and join in the brand new scene. For example, if the first two actors are involved in a scene depicting two bank robbers, the third actor can enter as Tarzan looking for Jane; the first pair of actors must immediately switch gears and work into a jungle-Tarzan scene. Although difficult, this variation is good because it forces the actors to act and react instantaneously without any advance planning. If the group tries this variation, the two actors already on stage might freeze momentarily while the third actor enters. This helps to break the momentum of the scene in progress.

Variation: Four actors are selected and numbered: 1, 2, 3, 4. The first actor starts a solo scene on a set the group leader has arranged. A couple of chairs and a small hand prop such as a newspaper usually suffices. The second actor, on a signal from the leader, joins the action; the third and fourth actors eventually do the same, until all four actors are on the stage.
Then, again on signal from the group leader, the first actor exits, followed, in accordance with a signal, by the second and the third, until the fourth actor is left alone on the stage and plays the scene as a monologue until the leader signals him/her to conclude it.

Variation: The process is the same, except that the events are those that might take place in a dream. Of course, this is an invitation for any sort of event or action: realistic or fantastic, logical or illogical. Radical changes in plot, voices, moods, settings and characters are all acceptable within the framework of a dream. Actors find this approach very freeing.

o

nce: Two actors go on stage. The group leader or another ...or "freezes" them into positions of action. The two actors stay frozen for about five seconds and then commence to play a scene to a conclusion. Positions depicting conflict or vastly different activities, levels or attitudes initiate the most interesting scenes.

Variation: Actors are also given ages and character types before the scene begins.

Group Improvs with a Given Situation

Performance: Two to five actors are given a situation, which may or may not include a specific setting or character types, and a short time to confer (30 seconds to one minute); and then they act out the situation to a conclusion. For convenience, the situations can be written out on index cards.

Sample situations:

- A student misbehaves and gets thrown out of class.
- While on restriction, teen-agers try to sneak out.
- Teen-agers go for a roller coaster ride. All react differently.
- Bank employees get caught in the safe.
- An airplane has engine trouble.
- washing windows on the 17th floor
- first day working at McDonald's
- inexperienced waiters in a fancy restaurant
- kids planning to run away from home
- Elderly people go birdwatching.
- Rookie firefighters go out on their first alarm.
- a hot-air balloon ride
- Small children go exploring and get locked in a closet.
- teen-agers being followed around by a bratty kid
- college students on an oceanliner cruise
- robbers breaking into a safe in a bank
- watching a scary movie on a stormy night

- Escaped prisoners stop for gas. The station attendant is old and very slow.

- Passengers on an airplane discover they are sitting next to a movie star or some other famous person.

- students in a science lab trying to discover new formulas

- Passengers in a speeding car are stopped by the police.

- Teen-agers sneak into the house at 2 a.m.; they were supposed to be home at 11 p.m.

- students called into the principal's office

- Riders get stuck at the top of a ferris wheel.

- An elevator gets stuck. Characters react in different ways: claustrophobia, impatience, heart attack.

- Kids are playing outside when one falls and breaks an arm. The others must decide how to help.

- Students on an overnight trip try to break curfew and sneak out of the hotel.

- New students are in class and brag how good their old school was.

- Two people discover they are going to the homecoming dance with the same person.

- Family members in a car are having an argument, and then the car runs out of gas in the middle of nowhere.

- A customer wants a simple haircut (or pair of shoes), but the hairdresser (clerk) wants to give him/her the latest fashion.

- Kids bring home a new and very unusual pet, but their parents don't want them to keep it.

- While playing baseball, kids break an old person's window.

- The brakes on a bus give out. On the bus are: newlyweds, a mother with a new baby, someone recovering from an operation.

- After coming home from a movie, a teen-ager invites his/her date in for a snack. Either younger siblings or a grandparent is still awake.

- While on a camping trip, characters hear on a portable radio that convicts have escaped from a nearby prison.

- Young interns perform a complicated operation for the first time.

bragging about what a good skier (tennis player, etc.) ..ᴗꜰ she is, that person is then invited to ski (play tennis, etc.).

- A kid tries to tell his/her parents about a misdeed in such a way they don't get upset.

- The passengers and captain of a boat learn there is a bomb hidden on it.

- A customer tries to return a defective item. The clerk refuses to believe that anything is wrong.

- Two astronauts disagree on how to decorate their spaceship to Mars: antique or modern?

- Several people have lied about their cooking skills and are now posing as chefs.

- camping out on a dare in a supposedly haunted house

- A child tries to make friends with a bad-tempered elderly person in a park.

- Campers hear funny noises and discover a bear.

- Astronauts on a trip to Mars discover they haven't enough fuel to go home.

- a family in a hurry to pack and leave for a vacation.

*Advance preparation: Have the situations written on cards that can be handed to the actors.

Group Improvs — Three Characters

Performance: A group of three actors receives a situation and three different characters. Each element can be written on an index card for convenience. The actors then perform a scene, tying all elements together.

Possible characters:

- juvenile delinquent
- grandparent
- matador
- surgeon
- dentist
- symphony conductor
- mechanic
- a nosy, half-deaf person
- farmer
- Indian witchdoctor
- fashion designer
- taxi driver
- alcoholic
- secretary
- parent
- baseball player
- child — three to five years old
- disco dancer
- drunk

- huge fat lady
- president of a large corporation
- soldier
- yoga expert
- ballet dancer
- school teacher
- cheerleader
- tired young housewife
- lifeguard
- airline pilot
- athlete
- child actress for commercials
- horseman or woman
- young out-of-work comedian
- snobbish rich person
- boxing champ
- mountain-climber
- shy teen-ager
- movie star
- karate student
- rookie surfer
- college student
- coal miner
- chain smoker trying to quit smoking
- 1940s-type gangster
- cowboy
- lion-tamer
- young child covered with chocolate syrup
- miser

Possible situations:

- in a jeep, on an African safari

- camping out

- taking care of the lawn on a warm summer morning

- on a sinking yacht

- in a hot-air balloon

- having dinner at a low-class diner

- working at McDonald's

- bullfighting

- driving a limousine off a river bank and into the water

- getting lost in a cave

- at a roller rink

- having dinner at a fancy restaurant

- stranded on a South Sea island

- checking into a hotel

- selling a used car

- hoarding money

- making an advertisement

ing a riot

- playing musical instruments

- painting pictures

- about to meet the president of the United States

*Advance preparation: Situations and characters can be put on cards and filed separately.

Improvs from a Given Situation

Performance: Individual actors are given a situation and one or two minutes to plan, and then they act out the situation to a conclusion.

Possible situations:

- a teen-ager trying to convince his/her parents that a girlfriend/ boyfriend is acceptable

- A young kid has been threatened with a beating by an older kid.

- It's the last day of school and a student is waiting to go on vacation the minute school lets out.

- practicing a speech in front of a mirror

- a benched member of a football team waiting for a chance to play

- the lone survivor of a shipwreck waiting on a lifeboat

- someone in a plane, waiting to try skydiving for the first time

- waiting to meet a blind date

- getting prepared for your wedding, just before the ceremony begins

- planning what to say to your girlfriend or boyfriend when you're breaking up

- an expectant father in the waiting room

- justifying a crime you've committed

- hurrying to get ready for a date for which you're late

- boy- or girl-watching at the swimming pool

- While on a diet, you are alone with a box of chocolates.

- someone preparing to ask the boss for a raise

- captain of a ship waiting for the fog to clear over dangerous waters

- It's the last day of school, and you are waiting for your grade card to arrive.

- passenger of a plane that crashes

- Your car stalls on the tracks. A train whistle can be heard.

- A tired parent comes home to a messy living room.

- going to a final exam for which you haven't studied

- a police officer staking out a murderer's home

- a teacher just before the bell rings on the first day of school

- waiting atop a burning building for the rescue helicopter

- a bank robber hiding out from the police

*Advance preparation: Situations can be written on index cards, to be handed to the actor.

Solo Improv with Objects

Performance: In this improvisation, the actor is given an object and must build a scene around the object. Any object available in the meeting area is sufficient: chalk, a newspaper, a spoon, a pencil, an envelope, spool of thread, cardboard box, piece of soap. If you have a properties collection, you can draw from that.

TMATTY (Tell Me about the Time You . . .)

Performance: In this exercise, the actor improvises a story with absolutely no preparation. Standing in front of the group, the actor is commanded by the session leader to "tell me about the time" the actor did something — usually something totally outrageous and unexpected — such as a girl turning down a date with Robert Redford.

The actor must attempt to begin speaking immediately and to not ever stop speaking. He or she should try to avoid delaying tactics like, "You really want to hear about the time I went out with Robert Redford? Well, I'll tell you all about it." The actor must also keep talking, no matter how far from the original subject the conversation drifts, until the session leader signals him/her to stop.

Suggested TMATTY's:

Tell me about the time you . . .

- lived on Mt. St. Helens when it erupted.

- were hunting in Africa.

- accidently hit the principal in the face with a pie.

- fell into a shark-infested swimming pool.

- went on your first date.

- got caught cheating on a test.

- appeared as a guest on the Tonight Show.

- travelled to Mars.

- were making obscene phone calls and one of your victims called you back.

- joined the CIA.

- were sleepwalking and walked across the street and raided your neighbor's refrigerator.

- went to a rock concert and the musicians played classical music.

- sneaked out of the house to go to a party and wound up being locked out.

- wore dirty jeans and a T-shirt to a formal party.

- ate six large pizzas.

- refused a date with Miss America/a movie star of your choice.

- jumped off the Empire State Building and landed in Texas.

- were attacked by a man-eating plant.

Variations: This exercise could also be adapted for use during production. For example, Anne Frank could be asked, "Tell me about the time you first learned that your family was going to go into hiding." Henry David Thoreau could be asked, "Tell me about the time you were put in jail."

REHEARSED PERFORMANCES

One Situation-Three Ways Scene

Performance: Actors, working in groups of two to five, will develop a situation and act it out in three ways: in pantomime, with dialogue and then "experimentally," or in some totally unusual, unexpected or untraditional way.

Examples:

- Using a train station as a setting, actors portray the usual characters and events of a train station at 7 in the morning: ticket-sellers, passengers, conductor, baggage porters. They first act out the scene totally in pantomime. They then repeat the scene with the addition of dialogue. The third time they perform, the train is a horse-drawn, excruciatingly slow train, described as the best the train company has to offer.

- Actors present, first in pantomime, then with dialogue and finally, sung as opera, the following situation: two thugs attack an old lady, who successfully repels the thugs.

- An auto accident occurs. An ambulance rescue is performed in pantomime, then with dialogue and finally, with the characters portrayed as different animals.

Preparation time: 20 to 40 minutes

Performance time: five to 10 minutes

Stage materials: chairs, small table, costumes and hand props as available

Suggestions for conducting the activity: Actors may not immediately understand how to treat the third version of the situation. Stress that the main purpose of the activity is to see and experience the differences among the three versions. The contrasting manners of presentation lead to spontaneous discoveries about plot development and improvisation techniques. Encourage as much freedom and experimentation in the third version as possible.

SAMPLE

Names of
Group Members: *Erik Drake, Keith LaRue,*
Maria Vincent, Don Belanger,
Dave Biers

One Situation-Three Ways Scene
(Activity Worksheet — one per group)

DUE: *Today!*

I. FOUR IDEAS FOR THE BASIC SITUATION
(Circle chosen idea.)

1. *classroom*
2. *✓family dinner table*
3. *bank robbery*
4. *pancake restaurant kitchen*

II. ACTION FOR CHOSEN SITUATION
(three to five sentences)

Class members enter, being a little rowdy. Teacher tries to keep order, assign work, stop cheating, etc.

III. THIRD VERSION VARIATION

Classroom is a fish "school."

IV. SETTING *Classroom*

V. CHARACTERS

teacher, four students

Three-Items Scene

Performance: Given the names of three normally unrelated items, a group of three to five actors develops and performs a short skit that logically incorporates all three items.

Example: Given "a baseball bat, a pair of ballet shoes and a jar of crunchy peanut butter," the actors develop the following scene: Members of the Little League Tiger Team are depressed — it looks like they will lose their last game, too. Coach confers with a few players. Suddenly, Sidney, the worst player, reveals a secret identity! By eating a spoonful of special crunchy peanut butter, he emerges from the dugout, dressed in ballet shoes — Twinkle Toes! He bats a homerun and dashes around the bases.

Preparation Time: 30 to 50 minutes

Performance Time: three to five minutes

Stage materials: chairs, small table, costumes and props as available

Suggestions for conducting the activity: This is not an easy assignment; results may be mixed. However, it is a good exercise in plot development and logic. Each person in each group should be encouraged to develop a scenario on his or her own. The group can then choose the best, combine ideas or perform each idea.

To prepare the actors for this activity, list items from famous fairy tales; e.g., a looking glass, apple and poison, from "Snow White and the Seven Dwarfs," or a red cape, closet and basket of goodies, from "Little Red Riding Hood." At first glance, these items would seem to have little in common, but a story, especially of a fantastic nature, ties them together. In this activity, the actors must develop a story from a set of items.

In developing the scenes, the performers can look at each item as the basis of a scene or as a guide to a setting. For example, a baseball bat can be found in a home, a baseball game, a sporting good story or at the bedside of a scared old lady. Actors can then ask themselves what stories could be developed from these settings, and how ballet shoes and crunchy peanut butter could be worked in. Similarly, ballet shoes can be found in a messy closet, a dance school, a shoe store; they could be carried by dancers on their way to a performance.

Suggestions for items:

- toothpick, mink coat, machine gun
- birdcage, dozen roses, snow skis
- hat box, bowling ball, baby blanket

- typewriter, boa constrictor, roller skates
- razor blade, diamond necklace, broom

*Advance preparation: Actors watch or read stories and observe the role objects play in a story line.

SAMPLE

Actor's Name: *Glenda Danner*

Three-Items Scene
(Activity Worksheet — one per actor)

DUE: *Today!*

I. BACKGROUND
(Actors interview each other, using questions below and noting answers on this sheet. Actors should leave extra room when they copy this sheet from the chalkboard.)

1. Give the name of a movie or TV show you have recently seen. List three objects that were important to the story line.

2. Give the name of a fairy tale with which you are familiar. List three objects that are important to the story line.

II. GIVEN ITEMS
(from card)   *mink coat, toothpick, machine gun*

III. THREE POSSIBLE SETTINGS/ ACTIVITIES FOR EACH ITEM

1. *mink coat: coat store; buying coats; movie star at Oscar night; rich ladies in coffee shop*
2. *toothpick: building a model; testing a cake; restaurant*
3. *machine gun: war trenches; terrorist hideout; guard house*

IV. SETTING *Bakery*

V. CHARACTERS
baker, rich lady, two terrorists

SAMPLE

[Three-Items Scene Worksheet, continued]

VI. POSSIBLE STORY

A poor baker is busily making a cake for his richest, most important customer. He needs the money a lot. Then the customer comes in — a rich lady with a mink coat. She has come to see how the cake is coming along. Suddenly, the bakery is taken over by terrorists with machine guns. They want to take the rich lady hostage because she has on a fur coat. (The terrorists don't like anyone who wears animal fur.) The baker then says he needs to test his cake. He goes over to get a toothpick, opens the oven, invites the terrorists to come look at the cake, and shoves the terrorists' heads in the oven, as in "Hansel and Gretel."

If-I-Had-It-My-Way Scene

Performance: Working in groups of two to four, actors 1
consecutive scenes. In the first, they enact a situation as it usually
occurs in real life. In the second scene, the actors portray the situation
as it would take place in their wildest fantasy, as if "they had it their
way."

Examples:

- In the first scene, a son asks his father for the car for the
  evening; the father, naturally, refuses to lend the car and reminds
  his son to catch up on his homework and chores. In the second
  scene, the father gives his son the car keys and $100, tells him
  to stay out until 3 a.m. and volunteers to complete his son's
  homework and housework.

- In the first scene, a sales clerk gossips with another clerk and
  is generally unhelpful and inattentive while a customer vainly
  seeks help. In the second scene, the sales clerk is instantly
  helpful, pleasant, informative and even directs the customer
  to a competitor for a better deal.

Preparation time: 30 to 50 minutes

Performance time: five to eight minutes

Stage materials: chairs, small table, costumes and props as available

Suggestions for conducting the activity: Actors usually respond
well to this project, with a couple of examples to get them started. You
may want to begin by citing examples of frustrations of daily life —
being bothered by younger brothers or sisters; being given homework
in all subjects on the night of the basketball game; going camping only
to endure bad weather, mosquitoes and the fact that many supplies
were left at home on the kitchen table; going on a boring date. Any
situation they've experienced which they felt they would have handled
better if they had been in charge, or which they could imagine as if
their highest, wildest expectations were fulfilled, will suffice.

Actors should rehearse both scenes thoroughly.

*Advance preparation: Encourage the group members to list situations where they felt they wanted things to be different; situations
with which they are dissatisfied.

SAMPLE

Names of
Group Members: Sarah Taylor, Tim Tressider, Tammy Barrett, Nikki Winston

If-I-Had-It-My-Way Scene
(Activity Worksheet — one per group)

DUE: Today!

I. FIVE IDEAS FOR "REAL-LIFE" SITUATIONS
(Circle chosen idea.)

1. getting a babysitting job, then being asked out on a date

2. having to wait in a long lunch line because your classroom is the one the longest distance from the cafeteria

3. arguing about which TV programs to watch

4. seeming to gain three pounds if you eat even one French fry

5. having a teacher who gives extremely boring lectures

II. FIVE IDEAS FOR DEVELOPING THE REAL-LIFE SITUATION AS IF I HAD IT MY WAY

1. calories are reversed — celery stalks are 500 calories, milkshakes are 25

2. scene takes place in a Dairy Queen

3. teen-ager orders everything on the menu and gains no weight

4. If you don't eat enough, you shrink!

5. get a modeling job at the end of the scene

SAMPLE

[If-I-Had-It-My-Way Scene Worksheet, continued]

III. ACTION SUMMARY — REAL-LIFE SITUATION

Two girls enter the Dairy Queen. Both are hungry, but they are on diets because spring is coming and they want to wear bikinis. Everything on the menu sounds wonderful, but they end up ordering plain patties with nothing on them and diet drinks. They discuss diet books and plans for exercising.

IV. ACTION SUMMARY — IF I HAD IT MY WAY

Girls enter Dairy Queen, again on diets, but allowable foods are now milkshakes and french fries and cheeseburgers with the works. They order a huge meal. They know unless they eat enough they'll shrink away to nothing. They also discuss how exercise puts on weight. Finally, another customer walks over and offers them modeling jobs for the summer.

V. CHARACTERS

two teenage girls, counter attendant, customer

VI. SETTING

Dairy Queen

Exposition Scene

Performance: Given a simple situation, a group of three to five actors presents the situation, and through dialogue alone, reveals the events that have led up to this situation. Through dialogue, information about characters, setting, previous action and plans for the future can be revealed. This process is called *exposition*. The actors then bring the scene to a logical conclusion.

Example: Given the situation, "walking through a huge bowl of whipped cream," four actors reveal that they have been on a visit to the Reddi-Whip factory. At the prodding of one of the four, they have left the group to explore on their own. They argue for a while over whom to blame for their present predicament.

Suddenly, they hear ominous noises — the vat is beginning to churn faster and faster! They try to turn off the machine, but succeed only in hearing the voices of the tour group. Quickly, the four submerge themselves in the vat while the group passes, and then climb out to join the group, hoping the others will only find them a little pale.

Preparation time: 15 to 25 minutes

Performance time: two to five minutes

Stage materials: chairs, small table

Suggestions for conducting the activity: A good source for situations can be found in the short-short pantomime activity, "Walking Through," on page 29. These situations can be written on index cards and handed to individual groups. In preparing for the scenes, the actors should ask themselves, "What events led up to this situation," and, to a lesser degree, "What is the outcome of this situation?"

Emphasize that the actors cannot act out the events that have *brought about* the given situation; they must begin the scene *in the given situation*, and then through dialogue, retell what happened before the specified scene.

*Advance preparation: If possible, collect scripts for examples of exposition. Most plays, particularly one-acts, are rich in examples of exposition scenes. The opening scenes of "The Ugly Duckling" and "Trifles" are good to examine. Actors can collect examples of exposition scenes from TV programs. Put situations on index cards.

SAMPLE

Actor's Name: *Harry Drexel*

Exposition Scene
(Activity Worksheet — one per actor)

DUE:

I. BACKGROUND
(Actors interview each other, using questions below and noting answers on this sheet. Actors should leave extra room when they copy this sheet from the chalkboard.)

1. *(if scripts are available)* In the first few minutes of dialogue, what do you learn about what has happened before the play began?

2. *(if actors have been assigned homework)* Give examples of exposition in movies or TV programs you have seen.

II. SITUATION
(from card) *Locked in a safe*

III. FIVE IDEAS FOR EVENTS LEADING UP TO SITUATION

1. *bank employee wanted to rob bank.*

2. *customer wanted to see safe-deposit box*

3. *custodian came to clean safe*

4. *bank president showing safe to important visitors*

5. *robbers have been locked in by clever teller*

IV. CHOSEN SITUATION *#2 (customer)*

SAMPLE

[Exposition Scene Worksheet, continued]

V. FIVE DETAILS

1. *customer very rich*
2. *prone to heart attacks*
3. *employee inexperienced*
4. *customer in a hurry*
5. *safe is sound-proof*

VI. SUMMARY AND ENDING
(three to five sentences)

They pile up the safety-deposit boxes and finally reach an air vent in the celing and meet some incoming robbers, scare them off, and get out.

Picture Scene

Performance: Given a picture of a situation, a group of three to five actors develops a scene. Before the performance, the actors display the original picture to the audience.

Example: Given a picture of two judges holding up cards that say *9*, a group of five actors presents the following scene: Two people are about to enter a competition of gymnastics or weightlifting. They have a nervous conference and we learn that their scores will determine which one will go to the Olympics. They are best friends, so tension is high. They each perform in turn, and each receives a score of 9. Then, to their dismay, a third party walks up and receives a 9.8.

Preparation time: 20 to 30 minutes

Performance time: three to five minutes

Stage materials: chairs, small table, props and costumes as available

Suggestions for conducting the activity: As the actors seek to develop action to go with the picture, ask them to keep the following questions in mind: (1) What happened before this picture was taken? (2) What is happening now? and (3) What will happen next? These questions should help them direct their thinking.

Pictures for this activity can come from a variety of sources; those pictures depicting action, conflict or unusual characters work the best. For longer wear, pictures can be mounted on pieces of construction paper.

*Advance preparation: Enlisting the help of the group members, gather appropriate pictures from magazines or newspapers. Pictures from newspapers are particularly useful.

SAMPLE

Actor's Name: *Charlotte Mendoza*

Picture Scene
(Activity Worksheet — one per actor)

DUE: *Tomorrow!*

I. BACKGROUND
(Actors interview each other, using questions below and noting answers on this sheet. Actors should leave extra room when they copy this sheet from the chalkboard.)

1. What picture have you seen in a newspaper or magazine that records a dramatic moment?

2. What happened just before the picture was taken?

3. What might happen afterwards?

II. BRIEF DESCRIPTION OF GIVEN PICTURE
woman and a child feeding a dog

III. THREE POSSIBLE STORY IDEAS
BASED ON THE PICTURE
(two or three sentences)

1. *The mother and child are poor and can hardly afford to feed themselves, but have found a stray puppy and have taken it into their home to feed. Then they discover that there is a huge reward offered for the lost dog.*

2. *The child has just brought this dog home and is feeding it leftover steak when the mother discovers them. An arguement ensues over whether to keep the dog or not.*

SAMPLE

[Picture Scene Worksheet, continued]

3. *The mother and child are feeding the dog just before an important dog show. The dog food is supposed to make the dog's hair shinier and heavier unfortunately, all its hair falls out.*

IV. CHOSEN IDEA

#3 - dog show

V. CHARACTERS

the mother, the child, the dog, the neighbor who recommends the dog food

VI. SETTING

kitchen

VII. ACTION
(four or more sentences)

Mother and child sit worrying about dog show and how to get dog ready for show. Neighbor stops by to borrow sugar; they ask her advice; she recommends a product, which of course she just happens to be carrying. The other two try it on the dog; neighbor leaves, but watches through window. Dog's hair falls out; mother and child become upset; neighbor confesses she has always wanted to get rid of the dog and its barking.

Living Newspaper

Performance: Using the contents of a newspaper article for a plot, actors develop and present a short skit.

Example: Using an article about a woman whose stomach pain turns out to be caused by surgical scissors left in her abdomen five years earlier, a group of four actors enacts the following scene:

Setting: a doctor's office, with a nurse as receptionist. A woman in great pain staggers in, complaining of a stomach ache. The nurse calls in a doctor, who questions the woman, bends her this way and that, is utterly confused, and finally calls in a second doctor for an additional opinion. They decide to take X-rays, and they discover the scissors. They promise to operate immediately. The woman agrees, making them promise to take X-rays before they sew her back up.

Performance time: three to five minutes

Preparation time: 20 to 40 minutes

Stage materials: chairs, tables, costumes and hand props as available

Suggestions for conducting the activity: About a week before the rehearsal and performance date, encourage actors to collect news stories suitable for acting out on the stage. Each actor should be responsible for finding his or her own article. A group of actors can then help act out each other's stories.

The news articles should meet the following requirements:

- A group of three to five actors should be able to present the action.

- The action should not involve too many scene changes.

- The action should not be boring (announcements about economic woes) or pointlessly gross or violent (a grisly murder).

- Ideally, the action would include an element of surprise.

Encourage the actors to expand the story, but at the same time, to try to capture the character of the people involved: the irate captain, the lost little girl. Remind them that the exercise is one in characterization, more than in dramatic plot. News articles are surprisingly flexible in absorbing extra actors, if the group is larger than the cast called for in the news article. For example, one bank robber can become two, etc.

Junior high-aged actors have difficulty making the original action of the news article clear to the audience. They tend to assume everyone knows what the article contained, and the scenes tend to be somewhat sketchy. Summarizing written information and presenting it in dramatic form is a very complex skill. It could well take an entire semester to teach such a skill. Therefore, it is usually best to allow a member of the group to read the news article aloud before the scene is presented and let the actors concentrate on acting.

*__Advance preparation:__ Actors should bring in two or three possible news stories, or you can collect some newspapers to bring to the session.

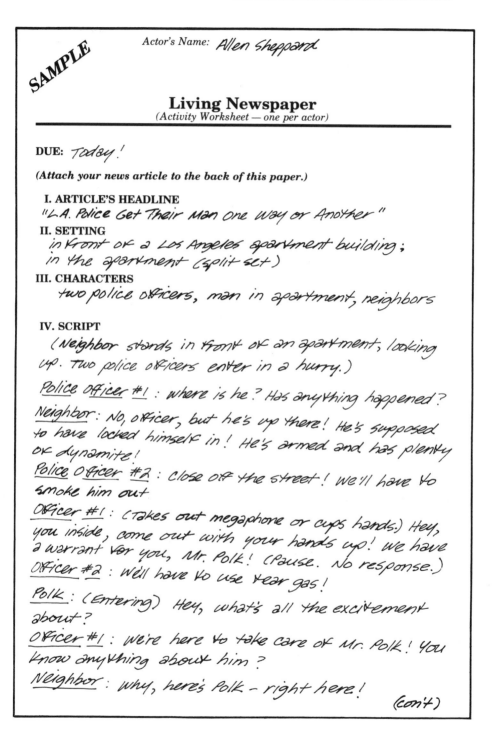

SAMPLE

Actor's Name: *Allen Sheppard*

Living Newspaper
(Activity Worksheet — one per actor)

DUE: *Today!*

(Attach your news article to the back of this paper.)

I. ARTICLE'S HEADLINE
"L.A. Police Get Their Man One Way or Another"

II. SETTING
in front of a Los Angeles apartment building; in the apartment (split set)

III. CHARACTERS
two police officers, man in apartment, neighbors

IV. SCRIPT

(Neighbor stands in front of an apartment, looking up. Two police officers enter in a hurry.)

Police Officer #1: where is he? Has anything happened?

Neighbor: No, officer, but he's up there! He's supposed to have locked himself in! He's armed and has plenty of dynamite!

Police Officer #2: Close off the street! We'll have to smoke him out

Officer #1: (Takes out megaphone or cups hands.) Hey, you inside, come out with your hands up! We have a warrant for you, Mr. Polk! (Pause. No response.)

Officer #2: We'll have to use tear gas!

Polk: (Entering) Hey, what's all the excitement about?

Officer #1: We're here to take care of Mr. Polk! You know anything about him?

Neighbor: why, here's Polk - right here!

(con't)

SAMPLE

[Living Newspaper Worksheet, continued]

Officers : wha—?! You aren't upstairs, with
explosives?

Polk: No! Really! There's nothing dangerous in
my apartment! I'll be glad to show you up!
(Group pantomimes climbing stairs. They enter
the apartment area and look around.)

Officer #2 : You're right! There's nothing here.

Officer #1 : Wait a minute! What's this?
Marijuana plants? OK, Polk, you're coming with
us.

V. ORIGINAL ARTICLE

LOS ANGELES (UPI) — Sheriff's deputies, told that a man "armed with ex-plosives" was barricaded inside his apartment, surrounded a block in South Los Angeles and ordered the suspect to surrender.

Deputies were summoned to the scene by county officials, who first tried to serve a warrant on Willie Polk, but were told by his landlord that he was inside the apartment with the explosives. Moments before the officers shot tear gas into the dwelling, Polk came walking down the street and asked the deputies, "What's all the excitement about?"

After the deputies told him they thought he was barricaded with arma-ments, Polk reportedly offered to show them the inside of his apartment to prove he was innocent.

The officers found no explosives. They discovered what they thought might be marijuana plants, however, and booked Polk on suspicion of cultivating pot.

cene

Performance: Given an ending of a scene, a group of two to five actors develops and performs the action that would plausibly lead up to that ending.

Example: Given the ending of, "throwing out a steak you've just cooked," two girls act out the following: Convinced they have no dates for the evening, they decide to cook a nice steak dinner for themselves. They do so, but the phone rings and it's the two guys they have most wanted to see. So, they accept the guys' offer of dates, throw out the steaks and hurry to get ready. (This is not the most practical ending, but it's dramatically effective.)

Preparation time: 15 to 25 minutes

Performance time: two to five minutes

Suggestions for conducting the activity: Give some examples of "thinking backwards" — which the actors will have to do as they approach this scene. For example, if someone walks in with a broken leg or a tear-stained face, what actions could have led up to this situation or ending? Then ask the actors to think about actions — more outrageous or seemingly illogical — that could lead up to the same endings.

For example, actions resulting in throwing out a steak could be:

- burning the steak
- hearing on the TV that certain steaks could cause food poisoning
- seeing the kitchen of the restaurant where the steak had been cooked
- having used the wrong seasoning
- seeing that the dog had eaten some scraps from it and had become ill

Each individual actor should devise a scene leading up to the assigned ending. The group can either act out each scene or act out a combination of ideas.

Possible endings:

- swallowing a goldfish
- making a quick trip to the flower shop to buy flowers
- burning up the homework you just did
- secretly letting a horse out of a fenced pasture

- tearing up a letter
- taking a big sip of vinegar
- putting a gun in a drawer
- selling a diamond ring your grandmother left you which you had promised never to sell
- putting your best friend in the trash can
- sneaking into a gorilla cage at the zoo

*Advance preparation: Actors observe endings to TV programs or movies. Put the above endings on index cards.

SAMPLE

Actor's Name: Dennis Schneider

Ending Scene
(Activity Worksheet — one per actor)

DUE: Today!

I. BACKGROUND
(Actors interview each other, using questions below and noting answers on this sheet. Actors should leave extra room when they copy this sheet from the chalkboard.)

1. Give the final action of a TV show.

2. Give the final action of a movie.

II. GIVEN ENDING
(from card)

cutting a potted plant to bits

III. THREE POSSIBLE ACTIONS LEADING UP TO THIS ENDING
(Circle chosen ending.)

1. just bought a pet rabbit and there's nothing to feed it

2. extra people have come for dinner and the salad seems too small

3. house guests who brought plant turn out to be a hassle

SAMPLE

[Ending Scene Worksheet, continued]

IV. ACTION SUMMARY

Two people are preparing dinner for some friends. They barely have enough, because they forgot to go shopping. The friends arrive, and they bring two extra people. The suggestion is made to go out to dinner, but the two hosts say there is enough for everyone. When they finally meet in the kitchen to discuss the problem, they decide to cut up a potted houseplant to make the salad bigger. They do so, and recieve compliments on the salad and everyone wants the recipe.

V. CHARACTERS

two hosts, two guests, two friends of the guests

VI. SETTING

living room and kitchen (split set)

ials for Products
⊥nat Don't Exist

Performance: Using the usual techniques of advertising, a group of two to four actors presents a commercial for a product that doesn't (yet) exist. The product can present an unusual, foolproof or bizarre solution to an ordinary or extraordinary problem.

Example: Three actors advertise the product, "Live Music." One, the announcer, comes forward, and addresses the audience. "Tired of warped records?" he inquires, pulling out a wavy record. "Tired of cassette tapes that come undone?" he sympathizes, unstringing a cassette all over the floor. "Tired of scratchy needles and static? We have the product for you — Live Music." The announcer points to a table, covered with a sheet.

He continues: "Suppose you want some nice, lively country music. Just push this button and" — as an actress dressed as Dolly Parton emerges from behind the table — "you have Dolly Parton in your living room!" "Dolly" sings for a while, and then the announcer pushes a button and she disappears. "Now, suppose you like classical music, so we bring you some Beethoven" — and "Beethoven" emerges, playing the piano. "Thank you, Ludwig. And then, there is rock music, and we have (name a popular drummer and his group) doing his famous drum solo!" The drummer emerges, begins and shows no interest in disappearing when the announcer pushes the button. The drummer gets more enthusiastic, the announcer more desperate. He finally admits to the audience that "there are a few bugs to be worked out, but get it — now on sale for $499!"

Preparation time: 30 to 60 minutes

Performance time: two to three minutes

Stage materials: chairs, tables, all available hand props

Suggestions for conducting the activity: Most actors respond enthusiastically to this project, especially with the example above. The easiest approach to this activity is for them to think of problems in their daily lives that currently have no solution, and to dream up the most fantastic solution imaginable. Parent problems, pimple problems, current fashionable "problems" such as weight and hairstyle, can all be solved with one new product that the actors dream up. If in the course of the commercial, the product backfires, the scene can take on a satisfying comic touch, but a twist ending is unnecessary for a good, entertaining scene.

All commercials have structures. To help the actors devise their commercials, review common advertising techniques:

- "before" vs. "after" (or cause and effect): Before using the product, Mr. X is lonely, sad and has yellow teeth; after he uses the product, he is popular, happy and his teeth gleam like pearls.

- product testing: Sneezing causes tissue brand X to disintegrate, brand Y to evaporate, but our brand stands firm.

- testimony: Announcer shows or interviews satisfied customers.

- weird product personification or association: Creatures leap out of toilet bowls, little old ladies with strange accents carry coffee cans, sports heroes demonstrate use of shaving lotion between games, or the product talks, sings, dances or turns itself into a little man.

SAMPLE

Names of
Group Members: *Kevin Turner, Shelley Lang, David Pfizer, Alex Garcia*

Commercials for Products That Don't Exist

(Activity Worksheet — one per group)

DUE: *Tomorrow!*

I. BACKGROUND

(Actors interview each other, using the question below and noting answers on this sheet. Actors should leave extra room when they copy this sheet from the chalkboard.)

What are the best and worst commercials you have ever seen?

II. IDEAS FOR PRODUCTS

(two per group member)

1. *homework machine*

2. *mood-changing device for phone — instead of customers calling because they're angry, they're all in a good mood*

3. *extra-whitening toothpaste*

4. *funeral parlor*

5. *instant weight loss*

6. *disguise for sleeping through class*

III. CHOSEN IDEA

"Sleepi-time class glasses"

IV. ACTION SUMMARY

Student enters, announces to audience, "Science class — and I'm so tired — if only I could sleep!" Man in trenchcoat and dark glasses appears, and offers student a pair of "Sleepi-times." He demonstrates that he is asleep behind his glasses.

(cont.)

SAMPLE

[Commercial for Products That Don't Exist Worksheet, continued]

even though he looks awake. student buys a pair and goes into the class. The teacher enters, confides to the audience, "I am really tired today — if I could just sleep through this lecture!" Trenchcoat guy reappears and makes another sale. Both student and teacher nod energetically to each other and fall asleep. Then the principal enters and discovers everyone sleeping. He is about to get mad, when Trenchcoat again appears, and offers him a pair of "sleepi-times." He accepts and goes to sleep, too.

V. CHARACTERS

student, teacher, Trenchcoat, principal

One Situation-
Three Attitudes Scene

Performance: Working in a group of three, actors present a single continuous scene that portrays three characters doing a single activity or facing a single situation. Each character holds a different attitude toward this activity or situation. In the course of the scene, each character (while the other two freeze in place) gives a short monologue that expresses his or her true feelings about the situation.

Example: Three characters buy tickets and board a roller coaster. The ride begins. Two characters "freeze" while the third delivers a monologue that shows that he or she is enthusiastic and excited about roller coasters. Then that character freezes and one of the other two breaks from his or her frozen position and reveals, again through a monologue, that he or she is scared to death of roller coasters and would prefer to be almost anywhere else. Finally, the last character speaks up in turn, revealing that he/she hopes to enjoy the ride, but is nervous about becoming sick.

Preparation time: 15 to 30 minutes

Performance time: three to five minutes

Stage materials: chairs, tables

Suggestions for conducting the activity: This activity is good preparation for a longer monologue assignment. Acting out an example yourself usually clarifies the assignment. Usually the monologues are too short, so you can make the assignment twice, or you can set a minimum length for each monologue.

Each person in the group should be made responsible for developing a situation for three characters, and each group should present all three scenes developed by its members. Stress originality; cheating on tests and first encounters with drugs or alcohol are popular, predictable choices.

*Advance preparation: Actors watch for everyday situations where people react differently to the same circumstances.

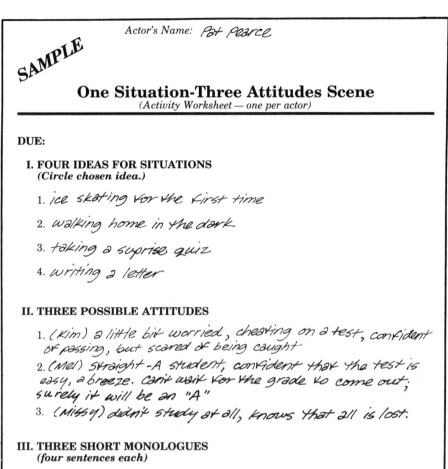

Actor's Name: *Pat Pearce*

SAMPLE

One Situation-Three Attitudes Scene
(Activity Worksheet — one per actor)

DUE:

I. FOUR IDEAS FOR SITUATIONS
(Circle chosen idea.)

1. ice skating for the first time

2. walking home in the dark

3. taking a suprise quiz

4. writing a letter

II. THREE POSSIBLE ATTITUDES

1. (Kim) a little bit worried, cheating on a test, confident of passing, but scared of being caught

2. (Mel) Straight-A student, confident that the test is easy, a breeze. Can't wait for the grade to come out; surely it will be an "A"

3. (Missy) didn't study at all, knows that all is lost.

III. THREE SHORT MONOLOGUES
(four sentences each)

1. (Kim): Ha, ha! This is easy! (Rolls up sleeve to look up answers) I have all the answers; they were on the teacher's desk! This will be sooo easy! Whoops! Here comes the teach! Better lay low (rolls down sleeve very fast, puts pencil to mouth, and appears to think out problem).

2. (Mel): Gosh, this is dumb! It's just like in the book. Everyone's worried 'cause they didn't study! (writes down answers very fast, smile on face.) Well, that's that! (walks up and puts paper smartly on desk, sits down and reads a book.)

3. (Missy): Oh no! I'm going to fail! I didn't study last night! Oh good, Mr. White's going out of the room, here's my chance! (Pulls out sheet of paper) Oh, these are for my other class! Here he comes again. There's no way now I can pass this test.

Solo Emotion Scene

Performance: Given an emotion written on an index card, the actor performs a one- or two-minute monologue. He or she should play a character who, in an appropriate situation, would express this emotion.

Example: Given the emotion "mischievous and prankish," the actress develops and performs a scene in which she spies on her sister and her sister's boyfriend.

Preparation time: 10 to 20 minutes

Performance time: one to three minutes

Stage materials: set props, simple hand props and costumes as available

Suggestions for conducting the activity: Stress the importance of believing in the emotion as much as possible. For more advanced players, stress a fully developed scene with a beginning, complications and suspense and a satisfying ending.

*Advance preparation: Actors list emotions they feel and others show in their daily lives. Write emotions on index cards for the actors to use. The selection from the impromptu solo pantomimes on page 28 is helpful.

SAMPLE

Actor's Name: *Vicki Peña*

Solo Emotion Scene
(Activity Worksheet — one per actor)

DUE: *Today!*

I. GIVEN EMOTION
(from card) *sulky*

II. THREE IDEAS FOR A SITUATION
(Circle chosen one.)

1. *You wanted a stereo for your birthday and didn't get it.*
2. *It is the day before report cards and you know you got bad grades and will be grounded.*
3. *It is the day of the dance and no one has asked you.*

III. TEN IDEAS FOR SCENE DEVELOPMENT

1. *Get home from school and wait for the phone to ring*
2. *Call friends and ask them what they are doing tonight.*
3. *Give reasons for no date — being ugly, it's your fate.*
4. *Try to console yourself.*
5. *Walk around grumpy and make a mess*
6. *Eat your troubles away*
7. *Say it doesn't matter, but it does*
8. *Say you're going to commit suicide. Decide not to.*
9. *Call up a guy.*
10. *Decide to go to the dance alone.*

Monologue

Performance: Each actor presents a solo scene. In this scene, the character speaks his or her thoughts aloud, talks to imaginary second characters on the stage, or addresses the audience directly. The scene should present an initial situation, complications and a solution. During the scene, the actor's lines should provide exposition as necessary.

Example: A chef with an exotic accent prepares and gives a cooking demonstration. She mixes various ingredients together with vigor, casually tossing out misfired concoctions and beginning anew.

She introduces a new cooking utensil — the oversized hypodermic needle, which solves any problem. No need for messy measuring cups — just insert the needle into the ingredients, draw in the desired amount, and squirt it out. By accident, she puts too much yeast in the pizza dough, but proceeds to bake it anyway. The dough pushes itself out of the oven and across the room, threatening to engulf cook and audience. Finally, she pulls out the trusty hypo and — *pop!* — deflates the overgrown crust.

Preparation time: one to two weeks (prepare at home). I suggest you collect the idea sheet and a rough draft of the script one week before the performance.

Performance time: three to five minutes

Stage materials: chairs, tables, plus all hand props and costumes available

Suggestions for conducting the activity: Give plenty of examples of solo scenes so the actors will fully understand the project. As a group, brainstorm situations in which someone might speak his/her thoughts aloud (a student who hasn't studied for a test; a teen-ager preparing to ask someone out; a patient in a dentist's office); or might speak to someone else for a long time without interruption (teen-ager explaining why he or she is so late; someone at a job interview; salesperson on the phone; a lawyer arguing in court); or might speak directly to the audience (demonstrating vacuum cleaners; dressing down a football team at half time).

Actors should avoid some situations. Counsel actors against portraying two characters in conversation with each other. If an imaginary character is also on stage, that character should have a minimum of dialogue. Scenes should not consist of lines like, "You say you want me to leave?" or, "You say the floor is wet and I should avoid walking on it?" Also, make sure they have plenty of lines — a monologue is not a pantomime.

Finally, a monologue script has the same sequence as all improvised scenes — an initial situation with necessary exposition, complications and a conclusion.

*Advance preparation: Make a list of examples of solo scenes. Collect examples to read aloud — Hamlet's speech in act II, scene ii, or Amanda's telephone calls from *Glass Menagerie* are both good. The examples on pages 136 and 137 can also be read aloud as examples.

SAMPLE

Actor's Name: *Belinda Davis*

Monologue Idea Sheet
(Activity Worksheet — one per actor)

DUE: *in one week*

I. TWENTY IDEAS FOR MONOLOGUES —
CHARACTER, SETTING AND SITUATION (OR ACTIVITY)

1. *vampire - coffin — thirsty*

2. *dog — city pound — about to be put to sleep*

3. *ex-Nazi - South America - sees a victim or policeman*

4. *pilot — over the Bermuda Triangle — engine starts to act funny*

5. *skier - Alps - stuck on ledge*

6. *astronaut — space — lost from main ship*

7. *Persian cat — cat show - about to be judged*

8. *football player - hospital bed - broke his leg before the most important game*

9. *Santa Claus — Christmas Eve, the North Pole — out of toys*

10. *young child - high dive - diving on a dare*

11. *monkey - jungle - flunked tree-climbing school*

12. *canoeist — city sewer — lost on a trip*

13. *young girl - beauty show — has come by mistake*

14. *old person — ocean — fishing*

15. *child — park — losing his balloon*

SAMPLE

[Monologue Idea Sheet, continued]

16. clown – empty circus tent – practicing an act
17. banker — sidewalk — taking a nap
18. bartender — bar — advising customers
19. mailcarrier — street — delivering mail
20. young child — utility room — helping with the laundry

II. POSSIBLE IDEA
child – in backyard – meeting Martians

III. TEN IDEAS FOR DEVELOPING POSSIBLE IDEA

1. Child is shot by Martian gun.
2. Child is captured and taken away in spaceship.
3. Spaceship breaks down.
4. Kid has a hard time talking to Martians.
5. Martians have no food that the kid likes.
6. Kid ends up on Mars.
7. Kid asks too many questions.
8. Kid tries to steal spaceship.
9. Kid wrecks spaceship.
10. Martians fix spaceship and rush kid back to Earth.

Sample Monologue Script #1

"No Respect for the Dead"

I never thought I'd see the day when I would be lying in a $5 coffin. I left my girlfriend $5,000 toward my funeral. Oh, well. Here come those guys who carry my coffin. I guess it's time for the funeral. Wow, look at this crowd. Let me count. Man, a grand total of five people. My girlfriend should be able to afford invitations. I wonder what she did with the dough.

Here comes the preacher. I guess everyone should stand up. Oh, yeah — that's in a court. Well, that's life for you: born one day, dead the other. Let's hear what the preacher has to say about me. Man, I've been to 18 funerals in my lifetime and they all started with the same line: "He was a good man." I was *not* good.

I wish he could hear me now. I'd tell him why I'm dead. Pot overdose. I'd tell him about the time I put 20 tacks in the vice-principal's chair. Heh, heh, he must have hit the roof. Those were the best 13 years of my life.

Oh, oh, here come those flaky dudes who carry my coffin, again. Hey, have some respect for the dead! Well, time for the Hertz ride. Hey, what is this? Whoever heard of going to a cemetery in a wagon pulled by a mule? My girlfriend sure spared no expense — with my money! What next!?

I should have known. Check out that plywood headstone with my name and everything printed in paint. Look at my girlfriend. She went and bought a mink coat and a new boyfriend with my money.

Hey, what am I doing dressed in white? I was in a black suit when I left the church. I think it's time to go to that big school in the sky.

— Nathan McCray, eighth-grader, 1979

Sample Monologue Script #2

"Babysitter's Delight"

(To parents, who are leaving) OK, 8 o'clock bedtime and a popsicle for dessert. I'll remember that. Bye!

(To kid) Hello, Johnny, I'm your new babysitter. By the way, what happened to your old one? She what? She fell out one of your windows and broke both her arms? How strange! Well, I'm going to watch some

TV now. Why don't you go play in your room?

Ouch! Johnny! Give me that stupid gun with the rubber-tipped darts! It's breaking my concentration on Starsky and Hutch! Ow!! Let go of my arm! You're going to break it! What do you mean, "good"? Why, you little brat — ow! *(Pushes kid away.)*
Now, go to bed! Oh, I forgot to give you your popsicle. Well, just a minute, and I'll get it for you. Oh! You have your own way of fixing it? All right, *you* can fix it. What are you doing? What is that gooky mess? You're planning to put that peanut butter and powdered sugar on your grape popsicle? Sick! You were going to put it down my back? You'd just better stay in here and eat it and clean up the mess!

Now, don't try to pull one of your temper tantrums on me! It won't work! What are you doing? Don't throw that slop at me! You're ruining my beautiful blazer! Stop! *Stop!* Now, get to bed. Immediately!

Whew, I finally got him to bed. Now I can finish my homework. What are you doing out of bed again? What do you mean, you can be bribed? What? Five dollars? Expensive little creep, aren't you? Oh, all right! Here!

— Donna Certo, ninth-grader, 1979

INDEX to ACTIVITIES

The exercise classifications in this index are largely self-explanatory. The index provides a quick reference — a loose, at-a-glance view of the activities. There's nothing rigid about the categories; index cards are certainly not mandatory, and any of the solo work could be assigned as homework.

All of the activities have been developed to be enjoyable, as well as to improve acting, with near-equal emphasis on "fun" and "actor training." A few activities, however, would not be too successful in a strictly recreational atmosphere, such as a summer camp dramatics day. Some of the others, in contrast, seem to develop some exceptionally entertaining results; hence, the categories "Emphasizes Actor Training" and "Emphasizes Fun, Entertainment."

Very Easy

Intermediate

More Advanced

Index Cards Useful

Leader-Directed

Noisy Rehearsal

Quiet Rehearsal

No Rehearsal

Good Warm-up

Good End-of-Session Filler

Best as Homework Assignment

Emphasizes Actor Training

Emphasizes Fun, Entertainment

Adaptable for Church Discussion

Adaptable for Social Studies Classes

Adaptable for English Classes

About the Author

Onstage, backstage and from the drama coach's viewpoint, Maria C. Novelly has been involved in drama since she was a student herself. Her interest in acting has been with her from Colorado to Texas, from Germany to California.

She earned her bachelor's degree in English from Colorado College and her master's degree from the University of Texas. She has served as a teaching assistant in the English Department at the University of Texas. She taught junior high and high school drama and English for five years in Germany, where she was also a drama coach.

In the theatre — both amateur and professional — she's done it all: actress, director, stage manager, technician, publicity director and scenery and lighting designer. In *Theatre Games for Young Performers,* her first book, Maria Novelly's love for the theatre and young people shines brightly.

Alphabet game

Group Improv - 3 char.

Order Form

Meriwether Publishing Ltd.
P.O. Box 7710
Colorado Springs, CO 80933
Telephone: (719) 594-4422
Website: www.meriwetherpublishing.com

TM

Please send me the following books:

_____ **Theatre Games for Young Performers** #BK-B188 **$16.95**
by Maria C. Novelly
Improvisations and exercises for developing acting skills

_____ **Theatre Games and Beyond** #BK-B217 **$16.95**
by Amiel Schotz
A creative approach for performers

_____ **Funny Business** #BK-B212 **$16.95**
by Marsh Cassady
An introduction to comedy

_____ **Improve With Improv!** #BK-B160 **$14.95**
by Brie Jones
A guide to improvisation and character development

_____ **Truth in Comedy** #BK-B164 **$16.95**
by Charna Halpern, Del Close and Kim "Howard" Johnson
The guidebook of theatre fundamentals

_____ **Spontaneous Performance** #BK-B239 **$15.95**
by Marsh Cassady
Acting through improv

_____ **Acting Games — Improvisations and** **$16.95**
Exercises #BK-B168
by Marsh Cassady
A textbook of theatre games and improvisations

These and other fine Meriwether Publishing books are available at your local bookstore or direct from the publisher. Prices subject to change without notice. Check our website or call for current prices.

Name: _____

Organization name: _____

Address: _____

City: _____ State: _____

Zip: _____ Phone: _____

❑ **Check enclosed**

❑ **Visa / MasterCard / Discover #** _____

Signature: _____ *Expiration date:* _____
  (required for Visa/MasterCard/Discover orders)

Colorado residents: Please add 3% sales tax.
Shipping: Include $2.75 for the first book and 50¢ for each additional book ordered.

❑ *Please send me a copy of your complete catalog of books and plays.*